Philip Hamerton

Playtime in the Primary School: Problems and Improvements

Phil Hamerton
Behaviour Support Service
West Base
St John Street
Mansfield

Playtime in the Primary School: Problems and Improvements

Peter Blatchford

London and New York

First published 1989
by The NFER-Nelson Publishing Company Ltd.
Reprinted 1990, 1991

Reprinted 1993
by Routledge
11 New Fetter Lane, London EC4P 4EE

Printed and bound in Great Britain by
Mackays of Chatham PLC, Chatham, Kent

British Library Cataloguing in Publication Data

A catalogue record for this book is available from the British Library

ISBN 0-415-09861-0

Contents

Preface

Education in Britain is now at a crossroads, with uncertainties and arguments over where the government's Education Reform Act is leading. The changes are fundamental, and cut right into the way schools are organized and managed, as well as the curriculum to be covered. On the surface it may not seem the most appropriate time to be concerned with playtime, which lies outside the mainstream curriculum and does not figure in the new Act. In fact I hope to show in this book that there are strong reasons why a concern with playtime in schools is overdue and necessary.

My own interest in playtime was something of a detour from my main interests. Let me describe how it came about.

In 1981 I began work with Professor Barbara Tizard at the Thomas Coram Research Unit, part of the University of London Institute of Education, on a major longitudinal study of children's progress in inner London infant schools. We were soon joined by our colleagues, Ian Plewis, Clare Farquhar and Jessica Burke. This was a large-scale project that investigated home and school factors influencing educational progress. We followed a sample of children in 33 schools, from their nursery class to the end of the first year in junior school. Chief among our findings were the importance of children's pre-school knowledge of reading, writing and maths on their attainments at seven, and the strong influence of teachers' expectations and children's curriculum experiences on educational progress over the infant school period. These and other results from the research are discussed in a book written by the team entitled *Young Children at School in the Inner City* (Tizard *et al.*, 1988).

The project was, I believe, an important piece of research, but, as others involved in longitudinal research will no doubt testify, the seemingly relentless following up of children can wear down even the most resilient researcher. It may therefore seem appropriate that my interest in playtime was aroused during long spells of field work to schools involved in the study. In fact I suspect that the seeds of most research projects – no matter how theoretical their orientation – are to be found in personal experience. In particular I remember one discussion in the staffroom of a south London primary school. It was after the end of the school day and I was there to talk about the research findings so far. The staff assembled only slowly in the staffroom, and I suspect most were tired and unsure whether the next hour or so were in fact the best use of their time. In the event, the results were I think of general interest, but for some reason playtime kept coming up as an issue, out of all proportion to its place in the research. There were graphic accounts of bullying and squabbling, and the difficulties of settling children down after the long break at dinner time. It unsettled and later excited me because I think I – like many in schools – had previously taken it very much for granted. I was aware of problems that could arise of course – who isn't in schools? – but perhaps for the first time I began to worry about how much we really knew about what took place at playtime, and, if there were problems, why we did not do something about them.

My interest was further aroused when we interviewed children in the study in their top infant year, when aged seven years. Their answers showed how much playtime figured in their experience of school. Yet when I looked to see what work had been done on playtime, I was surprised to find very little. If questioned, teachers, administrators and researchers would no doubt own to the importance of playtime – and indeed might well recount anecdotes from their own or their children's experience – and yet in their professional capacity all seem to have collaborated in a neglect of this part of the school day.

I was therefore very pleased when the opportunity arose to follow up results from the longitudinal study and look more closely at playtime. The aim was twofold: first, to identify with primary school teachers problems that arise, and secondly to document ways playtime could be improved. The research took place at Thomas Coram Research Unit from October 1987 to September 1988. This book is an account of that inquiry and my reflection on it.

Given that the research funding was only available for one year, and was for only one researcher, there were clearly constraints on what could be covered. The general aim was simple: to visit and discuss playtime with as many people as possible in the time available. The visits were restricted to the south east, in order that they could be visited daily from Thomas Coram Research Unit. Although contacts were made elsewhere by telephone, there were no doubt important debates and initiatives in other parts of the country that were not heard about.

Schools were not chosen on a random basis, but – quite the contrary – were deliberately selected, and self-selected, for the most part for the very reason that staff there had a particular interest in, and something to say about, playtime. This clearly limits the generalizability of views heard. But, at this stage, and given the limited resources available, it was felt to be the appropriate strategy. The aim was not so much the calculation of quantitative trends, as the identification of main themes.

There were several sources of information. In the first place, approaches were made to officials in Local Education Authorities in the south-east of England, informing them of our interest in playtime, and asking to be put in touch with staff in schools where issues concerning playtime had been identified, and/or where plans were being implemented to improve playtime. The aim was to visit about six primary schools in each LEA which had an interest in playtime. In this way, schools were visited in Barking, Berkshire, Brent, Croydon, Ealing, Enfield, Haringey, Hounslow, ILEA, Merton, Redbridge, Richmond and Surrey.

In addition, contacts were made with staff in organizations that have an interest in playtime, for example the DES, National Playing Fields Association, Interaction, Urban Spaces Scheme, Islington Schools Environment Project, Learning through Landscapes and teaching organizations. Other useful contacts with heads, teachers and LEA advisors came about as a result of responses to articles in the educational press about the research.

In discussions, a set of topics were covered and answers recorded verbatim. No attempt was made to standardize questions, and discussion was steered to the particular problems, arrangements, plans and initiatives that were of relevance to each school.

Acknowledgements

The original research was funded by the Economic and Social Research Council as part of a grant to the Thomas Coram Research Unit as a Designated Research Centre. It was because of the continuity of funds provided by this contract that it was possible to conduct a year-long study on playtime. I wish to thank the ESRC for their financial support.

During the research I spoke about playtime to many people. I want to thank them very much. I felt stimulated and wiser after each visit. I have done my best to report their views verbatim. Let me apologise now for any inaccuracies they may find.

It is my pleasure to thank Barbara Tizard and Peter Moss at Thomas Coram, and Jeff Dunn, head of Geoffrey Field Junior School in Reading, for their helpful comments on an earlier draft of this book.

I also wish to thank Maria Harrison and Olwen Davies for their speedy and efficient work on the manuscript. Lynette Koh is to be thanked for transferring the text from disks produced on my word processor at home to the much grander (but largely incompatible) system at Thomas Coram.

I would also like to express my thanks to NFER-NELSON, and in particular Roda Morrison, for their encouragement.

I am pleased to reveal my great debt to staff and pupils of Eardley Infant School in Streatham, and in particular Mrs Parker and Barbara Hawkins. Writing a book is a necessarily insular activity and my weekly visits there, and the welcome I received, were an important corrective, as well as a reminder of how good infant schools can be. They may recognize some descriptions in this book!

And finally I want to thank my daughter Kate who, although too young to be at school, made playtime at home such a rewarding experience.

1
Introduction

It is a rectangular shape, perhaps 100 metres long, nearly square, but with a small additional section that leads to the school entrances. It is surfaced in a grey asphalt, and is bordered by two high external walls, part of the school building, and a fence – on the other side of which lies the junior playground. Part of the fence is obscured by a large shed, with a high roof and a long wooden bench. There are six small trees, seemingly growing out of the asphalt, evenly spaced apart in a line a little in front of one external wall. They are circled at the base by newly built wooden slatted seats. Around the edges, and against the walls, are a number of garden benches. There is an iron gate leading to the street, near the end of one of the external walls, and, just inside, and against the adjoining wall, are two glass-fronted notice boards with messages for parents about forthcoming events. There is a lorry tyre in one corner, painted white, and full with flowers in bloom. Diagonally across the playground, and so near the school entrance, is a rectangular flower bed, neatly weeded, and also full of flowers and plants in bloom.

On the asphalt are a number of faded game markings in white and yellow paint. There is one for hopscotch, one for snakes and ladders, a snail shape broken into segments with number symbols inside, and a large irregular oval shape, in wavy parallel lines.

For the observer these physical features are difficult to take in because the eye is most attracted by the intense and varied activities of the 160 children. At first, the degree of seemingly uncoordinated movement is discordant and unsettling to the eye, and it takes a while before separate groups can be picked out, and some semblance of order found in the scene. Some of the activities of the children can be named with a fair degree of confidence. There are several girls with skipping ropes, showing each other how many times they can skip through the rope before it catches their heels and falls at their feet. There is a group of boys jumping on each other's backs and running after each other. They could be fighting, though presumably not because they are laughing and shouting excitedly. There are several other groups, and several pairs of boys who seem to be doing much the same kind of thing elsewhere. Against the fence there stands a line of children looking through at the junior children on the other side. Full size plastic footballs can be seen over the fence rising at intervals into the air. This, and the way the infant children pounce on the occasional ball that comes over the fence, makes the absence of balls on this side of the fence very apparent. They are presumably banned on this side. There are two girls skipping on the hopscotch design, but that appears to be the only game marking that is being used. Here and there are small groups of children clustered around the benches, some sitting, and some standing. There is suddenly great commotion, and a group grows around one of the trees. It turns out to be a large caterpillar climbing the trunk. Seconds later there is another gathering of children and much excitement near the notice boards. The one teacher on duty walks over to see what the fuss is about, accompanied by the six or so children who have hung around her since they came out. On inspection, it turns out to be a small hole in the asphalt.

But that leaves a large section of the children, whose activity cannot easily be named. Some do not seem to be doing anything at all – just ambling or standing around. Groups of children form loosely for a few moments and then break up, only to reform briefly again in different combinations. They seem to be engaged in some kind of chasing game, but it does not have a clear pattern. In contrast, others seem deeply engrossed in an activity which seems to make sense to them, though the rules are unknown to the observer. The observer asks a nearby child what they are doing. A bewildering list of names comes back. It includes: 'Daddies and mummies', 'Peep behind the curtain', 'Poor Danny is a weeping',

'Feet of London'. The observer asks how the last one is played. Other children join in to tell how it goes. They are clearly unused to explaining their games, and not all of what they say is intelligible. But the basic idea seems clear enough. You have to sit on the ground and if your feet touch the ground you are 'it'.

And so the activity goes on. The observer realizes, in struggling to hear what a child is saying, just how noisy it is. The observer, like the teacher, has a group of children hanging around, some explaining how things work, others voicing items of news with great gusto, and a few others who just seem to want to stand close by. Thinking about these rather lost children, alerts the observer to other children who stand listless and until then unnoticed against the walls and on the benches. But the observer turns away quickly to intervene in a conflict between two boys that seems to be brewing up out of what started out as a game. 'You have to watch those two', says the teacher, as the two are encouraged to go their separate ways, 'they either love or hate each other'.

Then a bell is rung and the children stop what they are doing and listen to the teacher shout instructions about going back into the hall. The sudden and well-organized shift to near silence and attention to one person, is again unsettling, considering the free-for-all that there had been a moment before. The observer joins the children trooping back into the school, and chats to some of them. At the entrance to the school it is clear that something is not right. A teacher stands with two girls, who are crying and holding their heads. The observer catches the teacher's eye. It is nothing serious it seems – just a clash of heads as they rushed to get through the door-way at the same time.

The reader has not been told the name of the setting just described but it is likely that all know what it is. It is actually a real playground, and an actual playtime, but something like it happens in every school, up to three times on every day, weather permitting. It is probable that everyone – even those who have not been near a school in years, and who might be bemused by the classroom environments inside the school – will recognize the scene from their own childhood. Probably, if they were to revisit their own primary school now, assuming it were still standing, very little would have changed in the playground. And they will probably still have memories and images of events that happened to them there – some pleasurable but perhaps more of them frightening. Indeed, the memories one has of playground experiences – of friendships, fights and games – can be some of the most enduring images of one's school life that one retains as an adult, sometimes more lasting than experiences within the school itself. If one thinks of first days at school it may well be a brief glimpse of a playground setting that comes to mind.

Playtime is, and has been in the past, an important part of school life. The school day is structured around the usual two short breaks of 15 minutes in the morning and the longer break at lunchtime. It takes up a surprisingly large amount of the school day. In a major longitudinal study of children's progress and behaviour in inner London infant schools, children in their top infant year were observed and a detailed continuous record was kept of how they spent their time – whether hearing a story, working on practical mathematical work on weighing, in assembly, reading to their teachers and so on (Tizard *et al.*, 1988). Children were observed from the moment they entered the class, usually just before 9 a.m., to the end of the school day, usually at 3.30 p.m. It was found that 28 per cent of the school day was spent in playtime, and much of this was in the playground. This was almost exactly the same amount of time as was spent in the total of all activities in mathematics, writing and reading. Only two per cent of the school day was spent in any form of reading.

Yet, considering how much time it takes up, playtime is largely taken for granted by everyone in schools. Staff in schools seem to have inherited playtime, much as they have the fabric of the building. And there is surprisingly little written material on it, either by way of policy or research. There has been a good deal of thought and debate about almost every aspect of primary education, and in many schools policies have been developed toward curriculum areas, like reading, maths, and science, and also equal opportunities and anti-racism. An important role has been assigned to play generally in children's social and cognitive development, for example, by psychological theorists as diverse as Piaget, Vygotsky and Erikson. Even more fundamentally, play is credited with an important role in the evolution of man (see chapters in Bruner, Jolly and Silva, 1976). Yet playtime has received very little attention. It could lay claim to being the forgotten part of the school day.

One of the most influential pieces of work that has been done on children's play is the book by Iona and Peter Opie called *Children's*

Games in Street and Playground (Opie and Opie, 1969). This is a detailed description of games children aged between six to twelve years play in the street, park, 'wastelands', and playground. Games from all over Britain are described in which children chase and hunt each other, try to intercept each other, hide and seek, race each other, hold duels won by a variety of skills, compete in trials of strength, dare each other to show their mettle, guess, for example, who has a hidden ball ('queenie'), act out particular stories, and pretend they are other people (for example 'mothers and fathers'). None of the games require any equipment, such as bats or balls. The work is apparently based on contributions during the 1960s from more than 10,000 children attending local authority schools. The games are named (over 2500) and grouped together. Some of the games are shown to be of great antiquity, and can be found in Elizabethan, medieval and even ancient times. The central theme is that left to their own devices children will play and pass on these marvellously colourful and resourceful games. It is a world apart from adults and they can only get in the way. It can help children gain control of their environment and gain knowledge of sensations beyond experience. 'In the security of the game he makes acquaintance with insecurity, he is able to rationalize absurdities, reconcile himself to not getting his own way, "assimilate reality" (Piaget), act heroically without being in danger' (Opie and Opie, p. 4).

More recently Sluckin (1981) observed children in two Oxford primary schools and also describes a rich variety of chasing, catching, seeking, racing, duelling, daring and guessing games and rhymes. He goes on to argue that playground activities serve an important role in children's social development. He argues that children are learning much during their play about skills essential to adult life – skills like influencing and changing rules, manipulating others, knowing how far to go. They are also learning about gender roles and power relationships appropriate to adult life in the society within which they grow up.

It is important to bear in mind the value of playtime. As Sluckin shows, it can provide a time when children can play with each other and learn games and social skills. It provides a time when children can be with their friends, perhaps not in their own class. Historically, its value has been to allow children time when they can let off steam after the sedentary activities of the classroom. It allows opportunities for physical exercise and fresh air. And, of course, it allows teachers to have a well-earned break away from the children and their classroom, when they can go to the staffroom for a cup of coffee and a chat.

However, there must be serious doubts about how typical the observations of the Opies and Sluckin are of playgrounds now. This was first highlighted for us when, as part of the longitudinal study of London children, referred to above, we interviewed children in their top infant year (Tizard *et al.*, 1988). Children were interviewed individually by a research officer. They were asked a set of previously devised and tried out questions and their answers were recorded verbatim. Included in the interview were questions about their experience of playtime. It was found that playtime could be a distressing experience for some children. Two-thirds of the children, girls more often than boys, said they were teased, and many clearly found name calling upsetting. And two-thirds of the children, boys more than girls, said they got into fights, though most said they did not enjoy this, fighting in self-defence, or because provoked and made angry.

Later discussions with staff in the schools which took part in the research confirmed this picture and highlighted some of the problems they faced, particularly in dealing with problems that had arisen at lunchtime. Some, it must be said, seemed resigned to the situation, but were also very aware of what was happening outside the staffroom window as they spoke. They would say, too, that the playground environment was unsatisfactory; it had nothing of interest in it for children to do, and despite recent efforts to tidy it up and plant some flowers, was visually very drab. And some – as the conversation on playtime developed – would be keen to know what happened in other schools, and whether anything could be done to improve playtime. There might even be alternatives to playtime, or different ways of organizing it. It is often when people take a fresh look at something that they know well, and yet which they take for granted, that one can see a sudden and fundamental awakening of interest.

It was in this context that enquiries were made about written material on playtime and that the paucity of information became apparent. And it was for this reason that it was decided to look more closely at playtime.

A main theme to arise out of this work should be stated at this point: there are problems with the way playtime is currently organized in primary schools, and there are signs that the situation is getting worse. We shall see that there are worries about children's behaviour in the playground. In contrast to the positive view that comes from Sluckin and others' work, there is a widespread feeling amongst school staff I have spoken to that children's behaviour is more aggressive and desultory than it should and need be. Though the murder in 1986 of a British Asian boy in a Manchester High School is thankfully a rare event, there are worries about the extent of violence, even in primary schools, some of which seems to be related to children's ethnic origin. There are worries that girls get a bad deal in comparison to boys, losing out on equipment, and being allowed less space by boys. And there are worries that young children in particular face problems in the playground, and that this may be growing because of changes in admission policies to school, with some children coming into school soon after their fourth birthday.

Parents, too, can be concerned about their children's experiences in the playground, and are understandably worried about safety in the playground, for example falls from a climbing frame onto asphalt. They also worry if they feel their child is being bullied in the playground.

It will be seen that there is particular cause for concern about the long lunch break. Because of recent changes, teachers now play much less part in many schools in supervision at lunchtime. Supervision now is often exclusively in the hands of largely untrained and poorly paid supervisors. This has been difficult for them, and the quality of supervision is not always adequate. It has also placed a great strain on heads, who can be the only members of the teaching staff on duty at lunchtime.

And it will be seen that some of these problems are more understandable when one considers the lack of interest and visual impoverishment of the playground.

It is particularly important to examine playtime at the primary stage. It seems reasonable to say that experiences in the first years at school will establish attitudes that will set the pattern for experiences later in children's school lives. And, as we shall see, much interesting work on playtime and playgrounds has taken place at the primary stage.

It would be disingenuous to claim this book has been written in a vacuum. It is written in the context of a growing concern with children's behaviour in school, evidenced, for example, by the setting up by the government in 1988 of a committee of inquiry into discipline in schools, chaired by Lord Elton.

The book is also part of a growing awareness of the importance of playtime in children's lives, and of its effect on the rest of the school day. And it is, moreover, written in the context of a growing consideration of ways that playtime can be used as an educational resource to complement the classroom. This can be seen in schemes to enhance the quality of play and cooperation in games in the playground and also in schemes that make use of the school environs as a resource for learning. There is also more thought being given to possible alternatives to the traditional fixed period playtime.

The aim of this book is to contribute to this revaluation by addressing issues and problems that arise out of playtime and identifying changes and improvements to playtime and playgrounds.

In the next chapter we will look at issues and problems concerning children's behaviour in the playground – at its nature, the quality of play, at racism in the playground, at factors that can affect behaviour there, and at characteristics of children who have particular problems there.

In Chapter 3 we look at what can be done to improve children's behaviour in the playground.

In Chapter 4 we examine more closely at lunchtime – at the problems of supervision, the extra strain on heads, and what can be done to improve the situation.

Chapter 5 looks at what can be done to improve the physical environment of the playground, for example by introducing equipment, making it more attractive, and rethinking the playground as an educational resource.

In Chapter 6 we examine possible alternatives to fixed period playtimes, for example cutting back on them, reorganizing the school day, so that they are scrapped altogether, and the so-called 'continental day'.

And in Chapter 7 some general conclusions are drawn and suggestions made for changes. Much still needs to be done and suggestions are also made for future work.

Throughout the book relevant research is discussed.

2 Children's Playground Behaviour: Issues and Problems

This chapter is about children's behaviour in the playground – what activities take place and the quality of play, what problems are presented to staff and what factors affect behaviour. It is very largely based on interviews with heads and teachers in schools, and must be viewed therefore as only one set of perspectives on playground behaviour, that warrants being supplemented by further research. A complete account would need to consider the views of dinner supervisors and parents, as well as children. Also, as we saw in the last chapter, schools visited were not a random sample and so no claims are made about the generalizability of views expressed.

But teachers' views and perceptions are clearly important in any understanding of playground behaviour, not least because, as we will see, they experience directly the effects of playground behaviour on school life, and also because they observe playtime at first hand, when supervising morning and afternoon play. Moreover, the aim of later chapters in this book is to describe improvements that can and are being made by teachers to playtime, and it is helpful to first present the context of issues and problems that prompted action to be taken.

The quality of play in the playground

It must be said that there is a pervasive view amongst teachers that the quality of children's play is not high and that there is a good deal of unnecessarily aggressive and anti-social behaviour. Much of children's play is seen to be physical squabbling, with much low-level physical play involving chasing and fleeing, jumping on backs, and fighting. Much of this is in turn attributed to acting out scenes from television programmes and films on video.

The report of one deputy head was typical. Because of concern within her school about the playground, she set time aside to look more closely at what went on. She was depressed by what she saw. She saw little constructive play. There was a lot of mindless running about, a lot of complaining and spoiling of other children's activities. Too much behaviour seemed gratuitously aggressive, or seemed little more than idling about without purpose. To this teacher it seemed clear that children were not playing in the cooperative and imaginative way she remembered from her own school days; in a very real sense children did not seem to know *how* to play. Incidentally, it is worth making the point that worries about playground behaviour were by no means restricted to schools in inner city or urban areas.

In other schools it is name calling and verbal abuse that is seen as the main problem. Staff in one school had set up three independent working parties to look at behaviour at school and all had reached this conclusion.

A survey of children's views about playtime, conducted for BBC school radio showed that children themselves were unhappy with playground behaviour, and that fighting could go unseen by teachers. The letters from children that accompanied the survey returns from schools paint a graphic picture: 'The first few weeks of term there was a fight nearly every break time. You nearly get knocked down every time someone runs.' 'Generally playtime is not such a happy occasion people make it out to be. Usually the weaker people get beaten up by the stronger people.' 'What teachers don't know is that a lot of bullying goes on.' (Quoted in The *Times Educational Supplement* (*TES*) 30.11.84.)

Sometimes it is difficult to know whether children are playing or fighting. There is a fine line between the two, especially with young children. And what can start out as a game based on Thundercats, He-man or Bruce Lee, where there are mock battles between goodies and baddies, can degenerate into open warfare. Much of this is seen by staff as petty, for example when a child misinterprets or over-reacts to a knock, but it can lead to fights, the forming of gangs, and threats from one gang to another.

In some cases the amount of aggression is a serious problem for the staff. One headteacher, new to a school, had been shocked by the level of aggression at playtime, in comparison to that in her previous school. Like others she noticed a lot of petty squabbling, but also biting and scratching. This was part of a more general climate of aggression that went beyond the playground. In one incident two mothers had fought openly outside one classroom. It was the head's impression that this kind of behaviour set the tone for the whole school because it set limits on what was acceptable.

There are signs of a growing concern with bullying in schools (see Tattum and Lane, 1989). Research on a representative sample of 1000 Cleveland children in their final year of primary school found that 23 per cent were involved in serious bullying, either as bullies or victims (Stephenson and Smith, 1989). In the majority of cases the bullying was said to be going on for at least a year. As the authors say, 'it appears that bullying is not a problem that "sorts itself out".' Attention is now being paid to characteristics of bullies and their victims (Olweus, 1984; Stephenson and Smith, 1989). It must be remembered, though, that bullying is affected by situation; one feature of bullying is that it tends to occur away from adults, often in the playground (Stephenson and Smith, 1989).

Staff in a junior school in West Sussex were worried about the behaviour in particular of one fourth year class, who had had a succession of supply teachers, and had become unstable and disaffected during the winter term of 1987. This had been manifested particularly in truculent non-cooperation with dinner supervisors, and had reached a crisis point of anti-social and aggressive behaviour. In January 1988 a decision was taken to move to the class an experienced teacher who had taught them in their first years of junior school, knew them well and had maintained the relationship with them.

As a starting point this teacher looked closely at the children's playground behaviour – where much of their anti-social behaviour took place – and spoke to the children about the playground. Again and again she heard the same comment: 'we're bored'. It was her conclusion that a large part of the problem was caused by children's lack of stimulation and direction in the playground. She was particularly struck by the contrast provided by school and playground environments. The classrooms and learning areas were stimulating, bright, flexible, and facilitated exciting activities and projects. In contrast the playground was a barren area, with nothing to occupy or stimulate children, and about which no thought had been given. She said, 'the playground is contrary to everything we do in school'. We shall hear more in the next chapter about how this teacher set about improving the children's behaviour.

Perhaps the most common perception of behaviour at playtime is of a certain degree of anti-social behaviour, accompanied by a belief that it is a containable, if hardly a good, influence. Several heads were keen not to give the wrong impression. One said, 'we don't have dreadful battles – it's not a battlefield. But it's a constant dripping tap of . . . so and so's done this and so and so's kicked my lunch-box'. Yet the head also added: 'But it means we have to counsel children, and it means we have to punish them, and that doesn't help relationships with teachers.'

It was a central theme of accounts from heads and staff that events and tensions created in the playground could adversely affect life in school. The head of an infant school put it this way: 'If we have an unhappy playtime the school goes up the creek.' In a similar vein the head of a first school said: 'If they come in after a positive experience they get on [in the classroom] in the right frame of mind, but if there's been a series of battles it is difficult to calm them.' Many teachers are aware of the time and energy that can be wasted after playtime trying to sort out problems that have arisen. This is especially likely after the long lunch break. One head labelled the first 15 minutes after lunch 'conflict resolution time'. And an experienced head of a primary school said: 'The afternoon is less happy for class teachers who have to start from a catalogue of problems which have arisen at lunchtime, when the class is laid out to do something pleasant. It spoils the quality of teaching.'

There would no doubt be a wide measure of agreement with these comments in many schools but it is also largely taken for granted – taken as an inevitable effect of playtime. One can sympathize with those who wonder whether these negative effects are justifiable. We look in the following chapters at whether they are necessary.

The demise of traditional games and rhymes?

So there was a general view that children generally did not play constructively or cooperatively with each other. One head said that, 'the skills of play with each other are very, very minimal, even though they've been through nursery. Oh they're good with construction toys and watching pictures on screens, but not playing cooperatively. There is a very limited amount of self-motivated games.' This comment about the lack of skill in playing in school was echoed in many visits.

It is related to another perception, expressed again and again during my visits: traditional games and rhymes, of the kind described by the Opies and others, and experienced by many staff in their own childhood, are, if not absent, then in steep decline. As one head said: 'I've never seen any traditional games and rhymes here. The traditional games are football and netball.' The head quoted at the start of this section said: 'They play the minimum of games in the playground. Traditional games and rhymes don't exist anymore.'

Some games were reported, for example 'In and out the dusty bluebells', 'Ring a ring a roses', 'Farmer's in his den', 'Hokey Cokey', 'Peep behind the curtain', 'Poor Danny is a weeping' and other skipping rhymes, and ring games. But the general feeling was that they were not common. One head said children have lost the 'vocabulary of play'.

Of course, not all playground games – for example, as described by the Opies and Sluckin – accord with romantic notions of children's play. Many are aggressive, and it might be argued that it is a reality of playground, and indeed adult, life that interpersonal relations can be abrasive and difficult, and children have to learn the hard way how to get on together. But it might also be true, as the Opies argue, that playground is an artificial and confined environment which encourages children, especially boys, to be more aggressive and belligerent. The skills learnt by children to survive there may not be positive ones, and some children can suffer at the hands of others.

There is, of course, a major question, here and elsewhere in this book, about the accuracy of these impressions of staff. The Opies were characteristically forthright:

> The belief that traditional playground games are dying out is itself traditional; it was received wisdom even when those who now regret the passing of the games were themselves vigorously playing them. We overlook the fact that as we have grown older our interests have changed, we have given up haunting the places

where children play, we no longer have eyes for the games, and not noticing them suppose them to have vanished (1969, p.14).

We will come back to this point below.

But if it can be assumed that there is some truth in the teachers' reports, it is tempting to ask why such a change in behaviour has occurred. One explanation is that children's lives outside school are now very different to those in say the 1940s and 1950s. A vivid sense of this change comes from the following account from the head of an infant school:

> When I was young we used to play in the street – skipping games, using a top. We'd get a washing line and all of us would jump together in skipping games. And we knew lots of rhymes to go with it. I can remember them now! There was a wide age range in the street – from four to 13 years – and so the older children passed on rhymes and games to the youngest. It was a sign of growing up to know the rhymes. Also games were seasonal – there'd be games for summer and games for winter.
>
> But all that has absolutely gone. How the children get to play at all is a mystery to me. There are signs on the estate saying they musn't play ball games. Parents understandably wont let their children go on their own to public parks and open places. This impedes their self-reliance and experience of play. Also TV is such a feature of home life now. It's a passive activity and the images are often adult ones.

And here is the view of the head of a first school:

> When I was a girl we made whips and played out in the road. There was only one car in the road. Now children don't play out. We had very little material. One ball between four, if we were lucky. We made a lot of it. Now there's a lot of material – magnificent toys. There's different values now. In assembly we hold up lost toys. They're not bothered. They say 'we'll go to Toys 'Я' Us' [a large toy shop].

The changes identified by these heads are frequently cited (see Baker, 1977, for a discussion from an international perspective of the effect on children's play of social changes). The central view is that, whereas once children played outside in the street, they now spend more time indoors, often passively watching television. Certainly it was the Opies' view that children learnt games from contact with their peers and siblings in the 'waste-lands' – places outside and away from the home and adult supervision.

Another explanation for the decline in traditional games is the relative isolation of children from an extended family. Some heads identified 'nan' as a source of information about games and rhymes, but for some children, especially on estates, she might live many miles away.

A rather less obvious explanation concerns the change in relationship between games and rhymes and the curriculum within schools. Rhymes and games of the kind described by the Opies seem to have flourished when primary schools were more formal. But over the past few decades many of the games and rhymes are encouraged and have become a part of the mainstream curriculum in the early years. In the Opies' descriptions of the games were in a sense an alternative to school and adult culture – they stemmed from and fuelled children's social relations. Now they are likely to be recognized as a part of a play approach to early learning, and rhymes, alliteration and word games now have an important place in thinking about early language. So there is not perhaps the same incentive for children to communicate games to each other and they will not have the same excitement and attraction for children. The Opies make a similar point:

> we feel it is no coincidence that the games whose decline is most pronounced are those which are best known to adults, and therefore the most often promoted by them; while the games and amusements that flourish are those that adults find most difficulty in encouraging. . . or are those sports. . . in which adults are ordinarily least able to show proficiency (1969, p. 10).

From this perspective it is perhaps small wonder that the exploits of He-man and Thundercats are seen as more exciting activities at playtime. Perhaps it is these figures and their exploits who are now the alternative to school life and something the children can identify with as their own.

This brings me to an important distinction. It may well be that there has been a decline in traditional games and rhymes, but this does not necessarily mean that there has been a decline in the general quality of play. It is too easy to dismiss games based on television heroes as somehow inferior to older, more traditional games. It is possible that the content of play has changed but that children can be as inventive, sharp-witted and as colourful in their games. As I have pointed out above, many of the games described by the Opies and Sluckin are physical and competitive and it is possible that at a glance they may be perceived as more aggressive and less rule-governed than as experienced by children. I got the impression from some heads and teachers that they had only a vague idea of what children did at playtime. It is difficult indeed for teachers to observe playground activity closely. Usually they are either on duty and therefore closely involved in supervision or else away from the playground in the staffroom. Observational studies in infant and junior schools have shown how different pupils' experience of classrooms can be in comparison to those of their teachers (Blatchford *et al.*, 1987; Galton, Simon and Croll, 1980). Part of the reason for this is that teachers have to oversee the activities of 30 children. How much more difficult it must be, therefore, to get a detailed and accurate picture of children's behaviour, when one has responsibility for supervising 200. It is likely that there will be a much stronger impression of disorder and physical movement than would be experienced by the participants. And, as one head said, people – and she meant school staff, both teaching and ancillary – have different thresholds for what counts as bad and anti-social behaviour. Some see misbehaviour where others do not. And, as we shall see in Chapter 4, teachers would not always pick up children for behaviour that irks lunchtime supervisors. One study found very little agreement amongst playground supervisors when asked to rate children's playground behaviour, and also very little agreement with systematic observations by trained observers. It was concluded that their perceptions of behaviour were based on a generalized view rather than actual performance (Murphy, Hutchison and Bailey, 1983).

But the issue is not so much whether staff are mistaken in the predominant view about the decline in the quality of play. The central point is that much more needs to be known in detail about children's behaviour in school playgrounds before any firm conclusions can be drawn, and indeed, before any organizational changes can be made with confidence. As we shall see in Chapter 6, one response to the problems of children's behaviour at playtime is the simple expedient of cutting back on time spent in playtime. But this is premature without first looking closely at what really goes on and whether changes to the playground environment or to playground rules and behaviour might be first introduced. We look at these possible changes in future chapters.

It is important to stress, while very much a minority experience among the teachers and others that I have heard from, that not all found the quality of play and traditional games to be in decline. The experience I had in a multicultural inner city infant school is instructive. The head was adamant: 'traditional games are not dead here! 'She mentioned some of the games, rhymes and songs she had heard in the playground, but she was not sure of the words and so we asked two top infant girls if they could help. We were treated, without any hesitation, to a faultless rendition of the song: 'The Sailor went to sea sea sea, to see what he could see see see, but all that he could see see see, was the bottom of the deep blue sea sea sea.' This first verse was accompanied by patting of palms and hands to foreheads in classic 'sailor looking to sea' pose. What was interesting was the way that subsequent verses changed 'sea sea sea' for 'doowup' and then 'Africa', the first accompanied by a vigorous swing of the hips, the second by a gentle sway of the hips. Other songs had other references to countries of relevance in this multicultural school. The two girls were for the most part in synchrony, though sometimes they argued over a line or action. Then four other girls were called over to help out with other games, e.g. 'Black, Black Magic', 'Hop, hop, hop to the lollipop shop'.

The performance was so impressive, that it was agreed with the girls that I would return the following week in order to tape the songs, so that I could capture a permanent record of the songs and study them in more detail. The actions were an integral part of the games and songs and so we made a video tape. The film was made in the school library and so away from the playground. It is therefore a matter of conjecture how much a part of normal playground life were these songs and games. But the experience in this school serves to show how easy it is to underestimate the prevalence and indeed the enjoyment children can find in games and rhymes. What is more, the games were certainly not learnt from teachers or in the school. The girls were in fact infuriatingly vague about where they had got them from – an experience I was to have in other schools! It appeared as if the girls learnt the songs from brothers and sisters and other relations, and, in the case of one song, from a girl newly arrived from Ireland. The words and actions were adapted to the lives and background of children in the school.

The way that children can adapt adult and sexual concerns to their play can sometimes shock. The two girls just described sung several songs that were ribald and which were accompanied by nervous looks towards the camera. The following game, described in writing by a child in a junior school, as part of a project on games played in the playground, is striking: 'how to play AIDS. One person is on it and counts up to ten and while hes counting up to ten we run away when he starts to run if he sees us he will try to catch you if he dus get you the only way to be safe is to say condom.' (Original spelling and punctuation). These and other examples should serve to guard against a narrow and romanticized view of traditional games, which may underestimate children and overlook play which is unsettling, perhaps, but also vibrant and sharp-witted.

Racism in the playground

Another aspect of playtime worries staff. Many have put a lot of effort into producing an atmosphere where groups of children from different ethnic backgrounds, and boys and girls, can come to respect and tolerate each other. And yet flashpoints can occur in the playground, where staff can have little contol over what goes on. It is likely that most teachers try to discourage racist and sexist comments in the classroom. As one head said, 'why, then, do we give over one quarter of the school day to providing opportunities in which they can flourish?'

The staff of this primary school were very concerned about tensions between different ethnic groups in the catchment area of the school, which found expression within school. In another school in a predominantly white working class area in North London, staff were concerned about the racist attitudes towards the few pupils in the school from ethnic minorities. This was a particularly settled community where some children were the third generation of the family to have gone to the school. Practically all the houses were council owned. The head said:

> They feel pressurised by Black Hackney on one side and rich yuppies pressing in on them. You can't excuse racism but you can understand reasons. There's a lot of racism, mainly verbal, in the playground. The strong dominate – very often boys. There was one Bangladeshi girl. Others wouldn't sit near her. The family moved to Finsbury Park. Racism is so deep seated here. Children pick up parents' attitudes. The National Front is very strong here.

There was a similar story in a school in an outer London borough which served a new, predominantly white, council estate. Again staff were concerned at the racism they encountered there. This area also had a very active National Front organization, which achieved a relatively large percentage of votes in the last General Election.

Given this background, the staff in this school felt that there were surprisingly few problems that could be attributed to racism. And indeed the general impression staff wished to convey was that there was generally little racist behaviour in playground and schools. The situation may no doubt be affected by a range of factors, not the least being the size of different ethnic groups in school.

Violence in schools and playgrounds has received wide media coverage but it is difficult to get reliable evidence on its nature and incidence. After the murder of a British Asian boy in Burnage High School in Manchester, a detailed enquiry was set up. It was concluded that the violent incident was to some extent racially motivated. Research commissioned for the inquiry, and conducted in three other Manchester schools, indicated that racial abuse and attacks were constant occurrences (E. Kelly, 1988). Children in the schools were seven per cent Afro-Caribbean, two per cent Chinese, and 11 per cent of Asian origin, and 22 per cent of 'Celtic' or non-European descent. Just over half the children were classified as 'English'. The majority of the 902 first- and fourth-year pupils, who responded to questionnaires, said that name calling was the most significant form of teasing and bullying – 66 per cent remembered being called names that made them miserable and angry. More boys (55 per cent) than girls (50 per cent) seemed sensitive to name-calling, and more blacks and Asians (76 per cent) than whites (64 per cent). It seemed as if the Asian pupils in particular suffered from name-calling by other pupils – 13 per cent above the average for all groups. It appeared that much of the name-calling was individualized – to do with details of personality and physical appearance rather than origin or neighbourhood. The one exception were words like 'yid', 'nigger', 'chink', and 'white honkey', which implied notions of group or community in terms of dislike. More Afro-Caribbean boys reported fights being picked with them than did other racial/gender groups.

Clearly the problem of racism goes beyond the playground, but this can be the setting where racist attitudes in children are most overtly expressed in schools, when away from adult supervision. Moreover, research on playground behaviour in Northern Ireland suggests that the playground is extremely powerful in socializing children into cultural identities: 'the playground is a forum where children in the province learn to be. . . Catholics and Protestants' (Austin, 1986).

This is a difficult and sensitive issue, and the reports described here can only be considered as a few perceptions on what is a complex problem. One would need, for example, to distinguish different degrees and types of racism. But even name-calling can be hurtful to the recipient and unexpressed resentment and covert prejudice between children can sour relationships within schools. More research is needed that looks directly at children's behaviour toward each other in the playground. This might be best explored in the context of a detailed observation study of playground behaviour. I will return to this point again.

The head of a large infant school in an east London borough was of the view that it was not generally children who showed racist behaviour, but parents. As a new head to a school with a quarter of the children from Sikh and Muslim families, she had introduced an approach to the curriculum and school life which was more overtly multicutural, for example in celebrating different festivals to the traditional Christian ones. Some parents had come to see her she felt, as a new head, in order to 'sus me out'. Two white parents had gone to her with objections that were racist. This school served an area of predominantly middle-class professional parents, which included the parents of Asian origin, and was heavily oversubscribed, and so the threat of children being moved to other schools was not taken seriously.

And the head of an infant school said: 'Here's a racist attitude for you. An Asian girl was told by her dad not to play with the rough black boys in the playground.' A similar instruction was given at another school by a white father to his six-year-old daughter.

Several heads were also worried about the attitudes of their lunchtime supervisors. As we shall see in Chapter 4, there is widespread belief that lunchtime supervisors do not always behave toward children in ways that teachers find professional, and in some cases they behave toward children in terms of presuppositions and hearsay. This might take the form of sanctions against certain boys who were 'known' to be trouble makers. It could also be based on children's ethnic background. One head said, 'more times that I care to remember I've found four black boys pinned against the railings. I say to the supervisors, I suppose all the other children have been sweethearts?'

To complete this picture, one also needs to consider teachers' own reactions. Research conducted for the Burnage enquiry (E. Kelly, 1988) found that very few pupils complained to teachers about name-calling, and this appeared to be because pupils did not feel teachers would do anything about it, for example, telling the pupils to ignore it. Also, teachers are not seen as entirely blameless. Seventeen black and Asian pupils stated they had been called names by teachers, and 34 pupils stated that they had heard teachers use racist names.

Parents and playground behaviour

Problems to do with the playground are of concern to parents. One worry, especially since recent television coverage, has been with problems of safety in playgrounds. We take up this issue in Chapter 5.

It was the experience of one head that, taking into account all their concerns, parents were mostly worried about playground incidents, for example, about their child being bullied. A recent survey in *Mother* magazine found that 38 out of 50 parents interviewed thought that bullying was the worst problem their child was likely to face at school (*The Independent*, 9.6.88). We have already seen that parents are also concerned about violence in the playground. A head said: 'Parents get uptight about playtime. They say their coats are dirty or the hood of his anorak has been ripped off. They get annoyed. They see incidents and take it as typical.'

Parents understandably are concerned about their children's happiness at school, and can learn, often in ways teachers do not see, that their children are upset about an aspect of school life – and this can be the playground. These fears should be taken seriously; teasing and bullying, for example, can make a child's life at school a nightmare.

For the most part it is possible for parents and school staff to work together in the best interests of the child. But comments from heads showed that there can be a conflict of view as well.

One difference of opinion concerned ways of reacting to aggression in the playground. Teachers take the view that the correct attitude for children to take in the face of intimidation and violence is to not react physically but tell an adult in charge. But staff reported that they were often working in the face of contradictory advice from parents. Parents, so staff felt, were too ready to tell their children to hit back. One school which was trying very hard to improve playground behaviour introduced a policy of non-retaliation and had had immense difficulties in persuading a generally unconvinced group of parents.

Some heads were critical of parents. The head of an infant school had this to say:

> Several parents were upset about fighting in the playground. I asked one girl in trouble 'why did you hit back?' She said 'my mummy told me if someone hits me, hit them back'. And this was one of the mums complaining about playground behaviour! I said to the mum if you say this to her how can you expect there to be no fighting? We try to encourage them not to hit back, try to get across that fighting doesn't solve the situation.

We have also seen, in connection with racist attitudes, that staff can find themselves working against a different set of values coming from the home. A head said: 'a lot of problems are because school and parents have not got the same standards. We are often at odds.' And different values are particularly likely to be evident with regard to behaviour in the playground.

In a similar way – and this is a complaint one often hears from teachers – some teachers complained that parents are not able to control their children in the same way as teachers. A head had this to say:

> Very often with parents playground behaviour comes up. But if I'm honest children are not well behaved with their parents. We've got lovely supportive parents. On a recent trip to the Commonwealth Institute we had enough volunteer parents' help so that there was one adult to three children. But their behaviour inside. . . the teacher in charge was a bit appalled. They let them dash around, running and screaming. They don't draw a line at all.

Such comments need to be treated cautiously; parents may be inhibited and unsure how to behave when teachers are present.

Some heads have taken direct action. The head of a Toxteth Infant school has recently sent a dramatic letter to parents asking them to act to protect their children's innocence before they become irreversibly corrupted. Speaking on behalf of the head on BBC lunchtime radio, a representative from the National Association of Head Teachers said that playground aggressiveness, foul language, precocious sexual behaviour, and mimicking of drug abuse were all evident and likely to come from the home – either from watching inappropriate videos or from copying behaviour there. The implication of this view is that the main responsibility for improving playground behaviour therefore lies with parents.

The views described here are only part of the story – one would need to look at the perspectives of parents on the situation and these might shed new light on teachers' attitudes as well as children's behaviour. And staff's perceptions of parental attitudes are not always the same, even within the same areas. What seems clear is that playground behaviour is an important concern of parents and school staff, but that there can be very different attitudes to how to deal with playground behaviour, and there is the possibility of much misunderstanding between staff and parents.

Factors that can affect playground behaviour

In some ways more interesting than general comments on behaviour, and more useful in attempts to improve behaviour, are factors identified by teachers that affect behaviour in the playground.

There was almost complete agreement that playground behaviour is worse during the longer dinner break than in the morning playtime. Many staff said that if problems are going to occur then it will be at lunchtime, and especially during the last 15 minutes or so, because then children are getting tired and irritable and can over-react. It was also widely reported that it was not only the length of lunchtime, but also the quality of supervision that caused problems. The problems and issues that arise at lunchtime are important, and specific, and we look at them, as well as possible improvements, in Chapter 4.

While there was much agreement that of the three breaks during the school day it was morning play that had the fewest problems, there was less agreement about afternoon play. Some reported no particular problems, whereas others found that children were more tired then and were more likely to overreact to trivial knocks. And the short afternoon break was seen to interrupt the flow and continuity of the afternoon's classroom activity, commonly leaving very little time to do more than have a story before it was time to go home. We shall see in Chapter 6 that in some schools afternoon playtime has been scrapped for this reason.

Playtime behaviour is affected by the time of year. Grassy outside areas are often unusable in all but the sunnier months and so everyone is confined to the hard-covered surfaces. Staffroom mythology has it that the weather is also a notorious cause of trouble at school. But many teachers are clear that cold and windy days can bring out the worst in playground behaviour. (We get most aggro with high winds and bitter cold'). Some children are certainly made miserable by cold weather and may not always be adequately clothed for playtime.

> When winter comes and it is really cold and when you can't stay in, it is like hours when you are out.
>
> In the winter we have to stay out in the cold and wet. It's all right for the teachers – they have a nice warm staffroom to sit in and have a cup of tea or coffee.
>
> We do not mind sitting on the steps to talk to our friends when it is warm, but when it is cold we would like a classroom to sit in please (Children's accounts to BBC Radio survey, see *TES* 30.11.1984).

As one head put it to me, 'you wouldn't send your own children out for 50 minutes in the cold. Not any more!'

If the weather is too bad then of course children do not go outside and this, especially at lunchtime, can itself cause problems. Paradoxically if there is anything worse in the school day than an aggressive and over-boisterous playtime, it is not being able to have playtime. There are particular problems of supervision then, and these are discussed in Chapter 4.

Problem behaviour can also occur more often in certain situations during playtime. Petty niggles can occur during lining up after playtime or when queuing up to go into the dining room. Staff in one school had gone to extraordinary lengths to identify where in the school most problems occurred and had literally restructured the school in the light of their findings. Many problems were found because several classes would file through one door and down one corridor ('like the M1'), and other problems were caused by children collecting in, and dashing out of, the toilets. Consequently the walls of the corridor had been knocked down to open up classrooms on to common areas, and access from school to the playground was made by building doors from every classroom. Screens outside toilets were also knocked down and toilets made smaller. The aim was to cut down as far as possible points of concentration of children and possible misbehaviour.

Stairwells, especially in large Victorian and Edwardian school buildings, can also be settings for confrontation. The head of a north London primary school said that it was a 'flashpoint' area, difficult to supervise, where children could be picked on and bullied.

Some staff also felt that the end of playtime – if signalled by a fierce auditory signal, like a bell or whistle – could bring children into school in the wrong frame of mind.

Characteristics of children who have most problems in the playground

Sex differences in playground behaviour

Perhaps the most widely accepted view is that boys and girls differ in their playground behaviour. As would be expected, boys are seen as more physically active and far more likely to be involved in fighting. Boys tend to dominate space in the playground, particularly because of football. Not all boys like football, and so this domination of space can be exclusive to only some of the strongest and oldest boys. If there is one activity in the playground that is mentioned most often as a cause of problems it is football. Many playgrounds are just not big enough to cater for a football match of the scale liked by children.

Research on children's playground behaviour suggests that pronounced differences between boys and girls exist, with boys playing more chasing and ball games, and girls playing more word and action games, or chatting in smaller groups (Dunn and Morgan, 1987). As might be expected, bullies and their victims tend to be boys. Moreover, bullying tends to be different for boys and girls; that seen among girls more often involves verbal bullying, while that involving boys is more often physical, or a combination of physical and verbal, bullying (Stephenson and Smith, 1989). One Canadian study (Beth-Halaachmy, 1980) found that, overall, boys spent more time alone than girls and also more time in large groups of six or more children. There was an age difference, though, in the kinds of activities they chose; it was only during the intermediate grades (grades 4–6, i.e., nine to 11 years) that boys began to spend markedly more time playing active games, particularly ball games, whilst girls tended to socialize with a small number of children.

This age difference is backed up by research in Northern Ireland (Austin, 1986), where it was found that boys and girls began to play separately between the ages of eight and 11 years. Girls of eight to 11 years were found to have a wider variety of games – skipping, ball games, clapping games, action games and ring games – that were often in small groups, were cooperative, and rarely depended on having a winner. In contrast boys games were more likely to be in large groups, often constituted as teams, and with an emphasis on winning. They were more likely to involve running, pushing and various forms of aggression. Austin argues that the playground reinforces traditional male and female roles; for example, rhymes like the following:

Keith and Caroline up a tree
K-I-S-S-I-N-G

First comes love,
Then comes marriage,
Then comes a baby,
In a golden carriage.

serve to reinforce the gender based roles of sweetheart, bride and mother.

Teachers can view differences in the behaviour of boys and girls as inevitable, and can learn to adjust to it rather than try to change it. There must be cause for concern, however, if boys tend to monopolize playground space, and girls come to accept this (as Dunn and Morgan, 1987, found). We look in the next chapter at some attempts to deal with this.

Age of children in the playground

Playtime seems to be more of a problem for some children than others. There can be particular problems for the youngest children in infant schools, especially now that children are entering schools in many authorities in the year in which they are five (see C. Sharp, 1988). Staff in infant and first schools can see the stress in young children associated with entry into school, and it is now well established that the problems faced by newcomers have more to do with playtime and lunch, than with adjusting to experiences in the classroom (e.g. Cleave, Jowett and Bate, 1982). One head of an infant school said: 'we had to drag children to the dining room screaming'. And one can imagine how frightened a child just into their fifth year could feel in a playground like the one described at the beginning of Chapter 1.

Children themselves are aware that young children can have problems:

> Being an infant prefect lets me see what really happens between infant and junior children. Infants come running in crying. Then you ask them what's wrong, 'a big boy hit me', they say.

> Most of the infants are scared to go out in the middle of the playground.

> I went round to see my sister and I saw little ones (just newcomers) being bullied by bigger ones. (Quoted in the *Times Educational Supplement*, 30.11.1984).

Certain children in school can also be the cause of most problems in the playground. It is often the view of staff that trouble stems mostly from a small group of disruptive children. A school in North London had particular problems with a group of five boys (two from the same family) who were persistently in trouble in the playground. The head said: 'they seem incapable of anything but inept and abusive behaviour'. Another said: 'The majority are not unhappy. It's a small group of children who are a problem – one group who are not happy and irritating to others, they're aimless.' These children were in two units for children with learning difficulties. Another head said it was usually only children from a nearby 'social priority' housing estate who were the problem. 'The estate is an appalling place – multi-story flats, family life breaking down. Drink is a real problem. Women too . . . If children came in and screamed and rolled on the floor it wouldn't surprise me.'

The more problems of an obvious kind caused by some children, the easier it is not to see the problems faced by timid and sensitive children in the playground. Some staff were aware of the problem. 'We are worried by quiet, terrified children with backs to the wall.' 'They are not all adapted to the playground. We try to pick up on the loners.' This type of reaction is particularly likely with newcomers to the playground. It was highlighted in an earlier research project of mine, which looked in detail at the behaviour of children, following entry into nursery classes in primary schools (Blatchford, Battle and Mays, 1982). Observations showed how easy it was for staff to overlook children who reacted not in an overt way but by withdrawing into themselves. This study was based in the classroom. The problems of such children, and the problems of identifying them, are likely to be more marked in the crowd and bustle of the playground.

There is another way that playground behaviour can be related to the age of children. We have seen already that there can be particular difficulties for the youngest children in school. There is some agreement that the top infant children, particularly boys, can be the biggest problem. A head said: 'The worst time in the playground is after half term [in the summer term]. The top infants think I'm the biggest. I'm going to Juniors. They get too boisterous for the playground.' Another head, in the same area, said she noticed the change in behaviour when children got to top infants. They become 'too big for their boots. They need squashing, reading the riot act. Once in the Juniors they're as meek as hell.'

Another head was also disturbed by the behaviour of top infant boys.

> It's the games boys want to play. For the most part this is fighting, violence, jumping on each other and 'killing' each other. There's so much fighting in the name of play, a lot of it connected with the television they see and comics they read. It all seems to be about goodies and baddies and no matter what one tries to encourage by way of peaceful activities and attitudes, most of the boys want to be like lion cubs, proving their physical prowess. This worries me. Some say I've got a hang-up about it. It goes right through the infants getting worse, so that top infants are a particular problem. The children will tell you they're only playing, but it can move into a real fight.

The same head was quite clear that behaviour improved in the Juniors. When asked to account for the change he thought it was probably because football had begun to structure the previously unfocused behaviour of the boys.

The deputy head of a middle school also commented on very noticeable differences in the playground behaviour of first- and middle-school children (the first school playground adjoined). Part of our discussion took place on a tour of the school and in a limited way we were able to test his observation. It was true, as he said, that the first-school playground seemed more cluttered, with a lot more movement, and coming together in temporary groups. Children in the middle-school playground, by contrast, were more spaced out, and there were more organized games like football and netball. Physical movement was more controlled and occurred in spurts. There was more standing and sitting.

In similar fashion, the head of a junior and infant school had watched the play of infant and juniors and thought that the juniors were more organized. Six or so children would spontaneously organize, for example a variant of British Bulldog, and would adapt the game to include new children as they arrived.

These reports from heads therefore suggest a change in playground behaviour between infant and juniors. It would be interesting to see if such a trend were found more generally.

What is more clear – and this is a main theme to arise out of this chapter – is that far more observations are required in order to clarify in a systematic way factors that affect playground behaviour, such as time of year, situations withing playgrounds and whether groups of children experience the playground in different ways. Particularly, more detailed information is required on aggressive behaviour in the playground – its nature, causes and development over the primary years. Recently the government has been moved to set up a committee of enquiry into discipline in schools, chaired by Lord Elton. It needs to be borne in mind that much disruptive behaviour has its origins, and finds expression, in the playground, and so such a study is important in an understanding of disruptive behaviour in general. There is an interesting contrast with systematic observations in infant (Blatchford *et al*, 1987) and junior classrooms (Galton, Simon and Croll, 1980). These studies show that disruptive behaviour within school is not common; a complementary account of playground behaviour is needed. And, as we have seen, more study is required of the quality of play in the playground. Many teachers will be the first to admit that they do not have a clear idea of what children do, though they can have strong views about it. They will not find much research that will help them.

3
Improving Children's Behaviour at Playtime

The school playground is in many ways an unnatural environment – crowded and barren of interest and apparatus. The behaviour that takes place there is not 'natural' play, in the sense that it is unaffected by many factors, some of which we looked at in Chapter 2. And playground behaviour can be affected by staff for the better. Steps can be taken to direct children away from anti-social and desultory behaviour towards more constructive and enjoyable behaviour. In this chapter we look at such steps. There are four sections: (1) ways of dealing with misbehaviour in the playground; (2) ways of improving arrangements for playtime; (3) ways of improving the quality of play, and (4) involving children in decisions about the playground.

Dealing with misbehaviour in the playground

All schools have ways of dealing with misbehaviour, of course, but one way in which strategies vary is in terms of how clearly they have been worked out. One head, on taking up her post in a junior school, found that the children's behaviour in school, in the playground, and on the way to and from school, was not satisfactory. She felt standards of behaviour had slipped and took very seriously the task of bringing about an improvement. ('I felt I had a job to do.') She instigated a set of clear rules to be observed at playtime.

1 feet to be always on the ground
2 no punching or hitting – go to an adult
3 no climbing on back games
4 no swearing
5 stop and think before acting. Ask yourself whether you would like it done or said to you. If not, don't do it.

A clear procedure was adopted to deal with misbehaviour. After a first offence children were reminded of the rules, and their name was put on an index card. This was then filed.

> If I see them again, I can look and know that we've spoken before. Then, depending on the seriousness of what they've done, they get so many chances. They are told when their last chance is up. Then I see their parents and we discuss the child's behaviour. On the whole the parents' response is positive. But if they don't come and see me then the child loses playtime – that usually brings them up. I've only had to exclude one child since I've been here.

The system operated in this school is given as an illustration of the kind of approach adopted in many primary schools. It was my impression that those schools which had what sounded like an effective system of sanctions (although I have no objective evidence to test this) had as a common feature a sequencing of sanctions, for example, discussion of correct behaviour, verbal warning, contact with parents, and finally being banned from play or lunch. This approach no doubt works to the extent that children are clear about what is required, and because of the hierarchy of sanctions develop a sense of the severity of wrong doing. But this approach on its own is limited, in that it only deals with constraining negative behaviour, and does not encourage positive behaviour. It must be considered, therefore, as only one aspect of an approach to playground behaviour.

Before we move on to look at a broader approach to playground behaviour we first look at specific ways some schools have devised for dealing with persistent wrong-doers in the playground. Bullying, as we saw in Chapter 2, can be a serious problem. Staff in a first school dealt with persistent bullying by first 'sitting on' the bully and then deliberately putting them in charge of the child being bullied. The aggressors were therefore given responsibility for their victim, and had the clear task of ensuring they had a good time at playtime. This was reported to work well. One can imagine the initial reluctance of the victimized child, but the unexpected assignment of responsibility seemed to effectively shake the bully into a change of behaviour.

Evidence from experimental work gives support to this strategy. In a study in North America (Fowler, Dougherty, Kirby, and Kohler, 1986) seven-year-old boys with histories of negative interactions were appointed as 'peer monitors' during lunchtime playtime, with the power of giving or withdrawing points for good or bad behaviour. It was found that their behaviour immediately improved, suggesting that the appointment to the role of playground monitor might itself prove effective in improving behaviour.

Readers particularly concerned with ways of dealing with bullying in schools will find much useful information in Tattum and Lane (1989).

A junior school in north London had problems with five boys who persistently misbehaved in the playground (see Chapter 2). The head devised a chart, a page for each week, and all reported misbehaviour was written down, along with the action taken. This action had the support of the parents and, four weeks into the initiative, the children's behaviour had improved. There was also a book in which all problems reported to the head were recorded. The head found this a valuable document because from it she could detect main patterns of behaviour over time.

Staff in some schools have been impressed by an article in the *Times Educational Supplement* (6.11.1987) which intriguingly suggested the use of yellow and red cards as a way of dealing with negative behaviour at playtime, rather in the way that football referees use yellow and red cards as a sanction in football matches. Staff at a middle school adapted the same system so that it had three levels. First, for minor misdemeanours, e.g. cheekiness and shouting, offenders were put on 'time out', i.e. they had to stand for five to ten minutes in sight of the playground but without communicating with others. Secondly, for serious offences e.g. disobedience, violence, swearing, racism, children received a yellow card which had to be kept until signatures for five days' good behaviour had been collected. Two yellow cards meant ten separate days of good behaviour was required. Cards were returned at the end of the lunch break and a decision was taken about whether a good behaviour signature should be given. Thirdly, a red card was automatically given if a child received three yellow cards, the result being exclusion at lunchtimes – the length of exclusion varying according to the offence. The scheme had only been in place a short time, but it was felt it gave a clarity and structure to sanctions that was of great help to lunchtime supervisors and to children.

Staff in an east London school also introduced the 'time out' strategy to deal with persistent fighting, in this case after the suggestion of an educational psychologist. The basic aim is to remove the offending children immediately and stand them on their own, away from the scene of the trouble, in order to deal first with the injured child. Later, after feelings have calmed down, the children can perhaps be brought together and the offending child encouraged to apologise.

Encouraging positive behaviour

The approaches considered so far are specific reactions to unacceptable behaviour. A wider and effective approach would also seek to encourage positive behaviour in the playground. The new head of an infant school had a particular interest in playtime. As part of her general approach to encouraging motivation and independence in children, she had introduced a positive reinforcement policy, within which, instead of the more obvious concentration on correcting bad behaviour, the focus was on rewarding and recognizing good behaviour. 'Always praise good behaviour if possible. If you are concerned with lining up then praise loudly those who are correct. Whisper to those who aren't.' If there was behaviour which had to be responded to, for example bullying by a group of boys of younger children, then negative reinforcement could be applied, for example by putting them on 'time out', as described above.

This method was in fact founded on well-established principles of behavioural psychology. Psychologists are well aware that a good telling off may be seen by some children as high prestige attention, and that punishment may in fact serve to encourage bad behaviour.

A recent study set out to apply behavioural psychology in a rigorous way in two special schools in Devon, in order to improve playground behaviour (J. Kelly, in press). In the first case study, three 11-year-old boys were offered an incentive scheme to help them improve their deteriorating playground behaviour, which included teasing, bullying, and abusing staff and other children. All methods of improving behaviour to date had proved ineffective. Discussions with the boys led to a programme which included a wall chart for each child which recorded good behaviour at break, and rewards in the form of sweets and much praise. At no time was disapproval or disappointment shown by teachers. Behaviour at playtime was observed before, immediately after and again six months after the intervention. It was found to improve greatly as a result of the intervention and to be maintained six months later.

The second case study took place in a co-educational day school in Devon catering for children with moderate learning difficulties. Junior playtimes were proving to be difficult, with an excess of fighting, bullying and general unpleasantness. Traditional approaches such as telling off and isolation of the children inside the school had not worked, and upsets at playtime often continued into lesson times and even on the bus on the way home. Clearly, existing management techniques were proving ineffective and breaks were stressful for staff and children. Baseline observations were conducted by the children, who were supervised by the teacher (who was also the researcher). The intervention took the form of rewards (sweets and tokens that could be exchanged for sweets) to children who did not engage in 14 behaviours previously identified by teachers and children as a problem, as well as a mention in the Good Work Assembly. Later, as a special incentive because behaviour was still unsatisfactory, each child caught not engaging in aggressive behaviour was given a formal letter to their parents praising their good conduct. It was found that physically aggressive behaviour decreased (fighting, punching, kicking and hitting) although there was an increase in verbal aggression, for example, teasing and name-calling (which the author thought might be explained in terms of a replacement of physical behaviour). The author concludes that: 'staff need to evolve a totally consistent policy for managing breaks just as they do for classroom activities'.

It is not suggested here that staff in schools would wish to emulate so rigorously applied psychological principles, and indeed, in the case of the work just discussed, some might understandably object to good behaviour in children being reinforced at the expense of their teeth! But the study does illustrate how behaviour can be effectively changed by non-punitive means, involving initial negotiation with children, constant encouragement, regular rewards and much praise and feedback.

General policies on behaviour involving the whole school

As has been said, specific policies to deal with misbehaviour in the playground are necessary, but they are likely to be most effective when part of a more general policy toward behaviour in the playground.

The head of a small rural school in Northamptonshire, as part of a course at Leicester University, produced a dissertation on the 'Quality of Lunchtime in School'. As a result of observations on children in the playground, discussions with children, teachers and ancillary staff, the head, on her return to school, instigated a number of strategies. They included an agreed code of conduct with children, lunchtime supervisor, teachers and parents, which included the sanction of three public warnings in one half-term resulting in a letter to parents. A venture considered a great success was 'the Zero Quarrel Option' which was carried out for the three weeks prior to Christmas. A quick check was carried out after lunch and those not having quarrelled were rewarded with a red star, thus ensuring praise for the majority of children and a reduction in petty squabbles. Other strategies developed in this school will be discussed in other sections in this chapter and in the chapter on lunchtime supervision.

This is an example of an approach that involves the whole school in the creation and maintenance of a policy toward behaviour in the playground. This is well-illustrated in the case of another school in a very different area of the country. It was the result of an interesting collaboration between Laycock Primary school in Islington, north London and the Department of Philosophy of Education, Institute of Education, University of London. Staff in the school were aware that playtime could be a grim experience for some children, and that playground experience affected everyone in the school. In the first place, a meeting was held for all staff (including ancillary staff whose time there was paid for by the authority) to discuss whether a code of behaviour was necessary. One problem encountered was that there were too many suggestions of rules of conduct and so later meetings tried to achieve agreement on the underlying principles for a code. Soon after, a meeting was held with parents to get their views. A draft document was then produced – 'Having fun in the playground' – to be sent eventually to all teachers, ancillary staff, parents and children, and it was used to encourage suggestions for improvement, and the inclusion of a section on sanctions.

A particular headache was deciding what to do about football. As in many schools, football was found to be a problem for children not playing – they could be hit by fast-moving balls, be pushed or scared by boys running, and find their space reduced to areas of the playground where football was not taking place. There was a strong impulse to ban football outright, yet it was also necessary to consider the rights, and enjoyment, of the football enthusiasts. The first draft code dealt with the football problem by banning it on Tuesdays and Thursdays so that the space could be used for other games such as volley ball, netball or handball. This rule was found not to work well, and was therefore toned down.

A revised version of the code was then produced and a whole morning meeting of staff was held, and a letter sent to parents, to prepare for its launch. The code was formally introduced at a whole school assembly.

It was as follows:

1 we will always be kind and considerate to everbody in the playground
2 we will look after the playground and make sure it is always a nice place to be in
3 we will share the playground space so that other games, besides football can be played
4 even if we are in the midst of something very exciting or important, we will stop and listen to any instruction an adult may give us.

The basic aim was not to make the code into a set of sanctions with which to constrain children, but to make the playground 'a fun place to be'. If anyone broke the code they had their name recorded in a special book. The book was reviewed weekly and could result in children missing playtimes or parents being invited up to school for their comments.

Several months later the staff felt confident that the code was working well, though they and the University staff recognized that they could not make strong claims about its success until a more formal evaluation had been conducted (see White, 1988, for a fuller description of this project).

One suspects in fact that it is not the specific items in the code that are effective. Indeed these will have to vary according to the characteristics and layout of each school. What is likely to be most important is the process of devising the code, involving as it did all members of staff, parents and children. Involving parents both by letter and in public meeting is important (see Chapter 2) and, as we shall see in Chapter 4, involving ancillary staff, as equal members of staff, is crucial. The willingness of the LEA to pay for their attendance is also important, and part of an issue we also pick up in Chapter 4. A major part of the process was identifying and raising behaviour at playtime as an issue. In other words, rather that responding to misbehaviour in piecemeal fashion after the event, and with rules and sanctions imposed on children and supervisors, a positive and very public effort was made to devise a set of principles that everyone played some part in the construction of, and therefore had a commitment to upholding.

Policies on behaviour for the whole school day

The involvement of the whole school staff is therefore important, but so too is a policy on behaviour in the playground that does not treat playtime as being different to behaviour during the rest of the school day. If the aim is to reduce anti-social behaviour in general, and encourage more responsible conduct, then we must affect events in the playground, but must not stop there. As the accounts so far have hinted, there has to be a policy for behaviour throughout the school day which is not constrained to either classroom or playground. Several heads who had thought deeply about this felt that an effective approach should not at root draw a distinction between school and playground. It is a corner-stone of good practice in primary education that one should work toward cooperative and independent learning in the classroom, but this is likely to be less effective if children have no sense that such concerns also apply in the playground. Similarly, even carefully devised sanctions for playground behaviour are likely to be more effective if integrated into a clear and positive stance on behaviour generally in school.

So two features of a sound policy toward behaviour in the playground have been identified: it must involve everyone in the school and it must be part of an approach to behaviour that covers the whole school day. It is easier for staff in schools to plan for such a policy with the support of the LEA. This is illustrated in the case of an infant school where staff focused on behaviour in school as part of an 'Institutional Development Plan' for each school, instigated by the LEA. It was felt that staff needed to clarify and improve behaviour in school before they turned to curriculum matters; that is, it was prior to, and would determine the success of, policies on reading, mathematics and so on.

The school served a Social Priority Area and had a high proportion of free school meals and high unemployment. About half of the children were from ethnic minorities. Through staff discussion and the setting up of working parties, they worked to develop a common code on behaviour and discipline based on respect for self, other people and property. The working parties all identified the main problem in the playground as verbal abuse and name calling, often of a racist and sexist nature, which had a demoralizing effect on children. It was decided, in common with approaches described above, that praise was more effective than reprimand. A policy was established, with the aim of 'being noisy with your praise and quiet with your reprimand'. They also worked out a system of sanctions which included a 'naughty seat' in both playground and classroom to which a child was sent so that they could view but not participate in what other children were doing.

Again, without evaluation of the scheme, it is not possible to say how effective it was. Certainly staff were not themselves fully satisfied; for example, in retrospect, given their belief that praise was more important than reprimand, they felt they should have first worked out a policy on praise before one on sanctions. There are also aspects missing, for example the involvement of parents. But in difficult circumstances, and with the encouragement of the LEA, the staff were able to see improvements in behaviour and get a clearer idea of what could be achieved.

Other schools in the LEA were working towards similar ends. Again, it is likely to be not so much the details of policy that are important so much as the highlighting of issues and the involvement of staff.

Equal opportunities and playground behaviour

In recent years there has been a growing, if sometimes controversial, effort to construct policies that further equal opportunities and anti-racism in schools. These are of relevance to curriculum matters in school, for example in worries about the way girls can become disaffected and underachieve in maths (e.g. Walden and Walkerdine, 1985). They are also of relevance to any approach to behaviour in school, and there is a special relevance here for behaviour at playtime, because, as we have seen, extreme forms of inequality and abuse can be found not in school but in the playground. In Ealing LEA, as part of an equal opportunities policy, school staff have been using the 'Genderwatch!' pack (SCOC, 1987) as a starting point for observing and altering behaviour in the playground.

It is not my intention, or within my capability, to deal here with the whole area of equal opportunities in schools. Instead, I want to look in a little depth at just one very limited, but important aspect of playground activity, for the light it can shed on attempts to change attitudes and behaviour in the playground.

It was seen in Chapter 2 that one of the most widely recognized problems in the playground is the unequal use of space and equipment by boys and girls. This is because boys and girls tend to play different games. As we have seen, this is seen most clearly in the case of football. It is extraordinary how important this one game can be in structuring and affecting playground behaviour. In a way it is a reflector of wider and deeper attitudes that divide the sexes, and it is little surprise that in most playgrounds the game is taken for granted by staff and children. But if football perpetuates divisions and inequalities between the sexes, it is surely appropriate for staff to consider the way it functions in the playground, in order to more sensitively approach children's attitudes toward each other.

Let us look at the approaches of teachers in two inner London schools. One teacher has recently written (ILEA, 1986) that the old arrangement of first come first served for footballs in the playground effectively meant that boys got all the footballs. So a start was made by making footballs available to girls. This teacher found that it was easier to change playtime arrangements if there was discussion with children that concentrated on the fairness or not of existing arrangements. This enabled boys to see that their monopoly of footballs and rough treatment of girls was unfair, although they did not apparently like to admit it. Change in playground behaviour, even of a limited kind, required constant supervision and did not come about easily. The teacher had to spend much time in the football area urging girls not to be afraid to tackle for the ball and also restraining boys from taking over the game. Not every girl wants to play football, of course, but with the teacher's encouragement and support some girls were joining boys in the game. In a way, encouraging girls in football helps them gain physical and psychological confidence, and can persuade boys that they do not have the right to take more space than girls.

A teacher in another inner London primary school took this a step further. This teacher felt it was important to encourage girls to play football, not because of any particular merits in the game, or because she wanted girls to be like boys, but as a way girls could reclaim space dominated by boys.

Her first step was to tell boys that some girls wanted to play football at playtime and should be allowed to do so. The boys were not happy, most believing that girls were unable to play. Reluctantly they agreed, a decision aided by the threat of having to alternate use of the pitch with the girls. A few weeks later the teacher told the boys she was going to put three of the best girls in the school team. As she writes: 'It had been my naive hope that they would be supportive to the girls and help train them.' But it was not to be. The team played a few matches and lost. The girls, so the teacher thought, did not play so well as in practice games. The teacher also noticed how the boys in the playground played around, rather than with, the girls, not involving them in the game or helping them improve. There followed a revolt by the boys who were convinced that they were losing because of the girls, and wanting the team chosen on merit. A meeting was called and it seemed the girls, too, had had enough of playing with the boys. It was decided therefore to have separate girls' and boys' teams, and to alternate use of the football pitch at playtime.

This teacher's experience is instructive because it indicates how difficult it can be to change gender-related behaviour. Many boys from a very early age have come to expect that they are better than girls at physical activities like football, and girls have not been encouraged or interested in playing. For both sexes, the experience of mixed sex teams was frustrating, and the boys were anything but encouraging. Changes to this situation will be difficult. At very least they will need to be considered at nursery level and at infant school.

The experience of staff in another primary school is also illustrative of the problems that can beset approaches to equal opportunities in the playground. The playground comprises one large and one small area. The school had a policy that big balls were only to be used in the big area. But because it was mainly boys who played with big balls this meant that boys had the large play area to themselves. The staff discussed this inequality in the use of space and had meetings with the children. At junior assemblies the head would chair meetings, and anyone was free to contribute. Their suggestions were written down. A decision was taken to use only large balls at morning play but it was found subsequently that in the afternoon the boys became bored.

So out of the meetings came a plan that in the mornings only girls could use the large area, and boys had to use the small area. During afternoon play they swopped around, so that boys could use the large area. This arrangement was tried for several months and then another meeting was held. It was found that all the children wanted to go back to the original arrangement where boys and girls could mix. The girls in particular were adamant that they did not like playing with the large balls and that they were not being penalized by not being able to do so. Not one girl voted in favour of the plan continuing. And so the school returned to the arrangement with large balls in use only in the mornings.

These difficulties indicate that an effective strategy on children's behaviour at playtime has to take on board in fundamental ways children's perceptions of their activities. This is another essential aspect of an approach involving the whole school, and will be a main theme of this book.

Anti-racism and the playground

We saw in Chapter 2 that racism is of concern, though the paucity of systematic evidence makes it difficult to get a clear picture of its nature and incidence. Yet it undoubtedly exists, as the recent tragic killing of a British Asian boy in a Manchester high school showed. It is known that the enquiry into the incident, chaired by Ian Macdonald QC, had strong words of criticism of the insensitive way anti-racist policies were implemented in this school. Though, at the time of writing, the full report has not yet been published, this has not stopped some national newspapers offering intemperate judgements on anti-racist policies in general.

Again, this is an issue that goes beyond the playground and will not be dealt with in any depth here. But it is important to say, to develop a theme of this chapter, that ways of dealing with racial abuse in the playground have to be considered as part of whole school policy on behaviour in school. The press response to the advance publicity given to the Macdonald enquiry was unfortunate. The problem of racial intolerance and violence certainly will not go away in the absence of specific policies to combat it. It is clear that it is the nature of such a policy that is crucial, and in particular its implementation within schools. It is, moreover, a policy that should hold centrally in view the less publicised, but still demoralizing, verbal abuse in playgrounds, because it manifests underlying attitudes that adversely affect the spirit of cooperation and generosity that can make schooling a nurturing experience for children.

It is my view that racism and sexism in the playground are best tackled by a whole school policy (in the two senses described above) that pays attention to specific manifestations of unacceptable behaviour and offers clear guidelines to staff, children and parents about what is expected. At heart this has been founded on a clearly stated moral position. One head said to me that one must make it clear to children that name calling, violence and verbal abuse are unacceptable. But it is also important to show children and parents that there is an alternative moral stance which offers non-retaliatory solutions to problems, for example, reporting incidents of provocation, rather than responding in kind. A climate must be created within which such non-violent responses are expected and respected.

Ways of improving arrangements at playtime

Staff and children in most schools may not have any choice over the size and overall design of the playground and outside area, but they do have the power to alter arrangements for how the playground is used. We saw in Chapter 2 some of the features of playtime that seemed to cause particular problems and we look here at some ways improvements might be introduced by changes to the organization of playtime.

Staggering playtime

It is probable that we do not give enough credit to basic environmental factors in playground behaviour. Most playgrounds in schools are crowded with children, with only one or two adults acting as supervisors. It may well be that at least some problem behaviour is the result of this overcrowding and thinness of supervision. One obvious way of drastically cutting the numbers of children outside, and also increasing the numbers of supervisors relative to children, is to cut by half the numbers of children in the playground at any one time; that is, to stagger playtimes, and have one after the other.

The head at an infant school was concerned at the number of injuries and quarrels in the playground and came to the conclusion that much of the problem was attributable to there being too many children in the playground. It is a large infant school with 310 children and it was decided to split playtime into two. The twelve classes were divided so that the top, and half the middle infant, children went out first, followed by the rest of the middle infants and the reception children. The head felt the benefits far outweighed the disadvantage of increased supervision. There were less accidents, less friction and supervision was easier.

As part of an LEA initiative, involving schools in the drawing up of an Institutional Development Plan, and referred to above, staff at one infant school decided to cut the morning and afternoon playtimes in two. In the same way as the infant school, just referred to, children were divided by age. It was the head's view that this, and the initial separation of the reception children (see below), had almost cut out problems during morning and afternoon play, though problems still remained at lunchtime.

In the last chapter, the worries of a new head to an infant school about the level and ethos of aggressiveness there were described. After discussions with staff she proposed a similar doubling up of playtime. Because staff were not happy about the increase in supervision this would involve, a compromise was reached: the afternoon playtime – when most problems were found to occur – was split into two. So far, behaviour was reported to have improved, though this school, like many in the same LEA, was being severely disrupted by industrial action at the time of my visit.

The drawbacks of this simple rearrangement of playtime will have to be considered; it means increasing the amount of supervisory duties teaching staff will have to perform, and it is understandable if they are unwilling to give up their own breaks. It is also not so applicable during the longer dinner break when, as we shall see in Chapter 4, different arrangements pertain. But it is certainly something staff in schools, especially with overcrowded playgrounds, might consider trying.

Four-year-olds in the playground

As we saw in Chapter 2, there can be particular problems for the youngest children in infant and first schools, especially now that children in some authorities can enter schools after their fourth birthday. A number of schools have devised arrangements to help newcomers adjust to playground life. Staff in an infant school recognized the traumatic time experienced by some new reception children, and so sent them outside into a separate area of the playground. In this way the newcomers were less worried by noise, and the sheer numbers of other children and rushing about.

Staff in another infant school were sensitive to the problems faced by newcomers, and looked at playground experience as part of a general policy toward the youngest children in school. A six-point plan was introduced with these children.

1 at first, attendance at school was on a part-time basis
2 they went home for lunch
3 a playtime rota was devised so that they went out separately into the playground
4 they had separate assemblies

5 special play equipment was provided in the playground, in a similar way as nursery classes and schools
6 they later ate in their own classrooms and each class was assigned one supervisor at lunchtime.

For children entering in September this plan would operate until the end of term. After Christmas they came to school for the whole day. Their playtime was still separate from the rest of the infants, but they could join the main playtime during the term. The aim was gradually to 'boost' up integration into the main playground, but if a child was not happy then they did not have to go out.

Other arrangements could include not having fixed period playtimes at first but taking children out when there is a natural break in classroom activities. Also, reception aged children could be allowed access to the nursery playground, if one is available.

That children are entering school at a younger age, is a matter of growing concern to staff, and it highlights worries about playtime experience. Staff at the school just referred to, and others, were forced into making new arrangements. They deliberately aimed to draw on arrangements more usual in nursery education; in a sense they were forced, within the infant school, to create conditions for a gradual transition from nursery to infant.

But special arrangements will always be a consideration with newcomers into school, even when they enter during the term in which they are five years of age. To the child new to school, playtime presents particular problems. Some form of initial segregation followed by a gradual integration into the main playground is always likely to be beneficial.

Mixing ages in the playground

We have seen that one way of decreasing the likelihood of problem behaviour at playtime is to decrease the numbers of children who go out. Another strategy is to alter arrangements for which children go out together. As part of a scheme in a West Sussex Junior school to improve playground behaviour, and described in detail below, changes were made to the mixing of the four year groups. Previously, first and second years had used the lower playground, and the third and fourth years had used the upper playground. A rotational system was begun so that at the end of each week the groups were switched around.

Week	*Upper playground*	*Lower playground*
1	4th and 1st	2nd and 3rd
2	4th and 2nd	1st and 3rd
3	3rd and 4th	1st and 3rd
4	2nd and 3rd	4th and 1st
5	1st and 3rd	4th and 2nd
6	1st and 2nd	3rd and 4th

The aim was to increase contact between different age groups and also to develop a sense of responsibility because the plan involved movement across the school grounds. The system ran for almost a term and was beginning to show positive results, but had to be suspended because the numbers of dinner supervisors were reduced and could not cope with the extra demands. The plan was to reinstate the arrangement for morning and afternoon play.

Staff at Ilfracombe Junior school in Devon closely considered behaviour and discipline at school and felt that many problems arose because of a conflict of interest between younger and older children. It was found that younger children, who had just entered the junior school, were intimidated by the size and confidence of the fourth years, and the fourth years could misuse this power. Two teachers – one who taught a first-year class, and one who taught a fourth-year class – evolved an interesting collaboration. Children in each class were paired so each child had a 'twin' in the other class. Some attempt was made to match pairs on ability and personality. The system involved collaboration within school on Friday afternoons; for example, the first years designed water clocks and the fourth years helped to make them, and the first years produced and showed a short play to the fourth years. But, in addition, it was found that fourth years now chose to play with their younger 'twin' at breaktimes. They were also found to devise games for them and deal with petty disputes, even intervening when bullying took place. For first years, playtime was reported to be more pleasurable and their play enriched under the care and protection of their older 'twin'. The fourth years were often surprised at how much the first years already knew and were satisfied to help the younger children, and so increase their sense of responsibility for them.

The system is therefore reported to encourage mutual respect and the development of meaningful relationships between children of different ages. The 'twinning' arrangement has been used in secondary schools to help the youngest children, and its use as a way of encouraging more caring relationships in primary schools might be extended.

Arrangements for time before school starts in the morning

In this book we are concerned with times children spend out in the playground. Apart from morning and afternoon and lunchtime play, children can also spend time in the playground before school starts in the morning. Staff in some schools identified this as a source of problems, principally because it was difficult to know when children would be there and to supervise. Bullying can occur at such times (Stephenson and Smith, 1989). It is not intended to say much here about this part of the school day, but it is worth documenting the approaches used in three schools.

The head at an infant school told me that behaviour in the playground before school started was not satisfactory and that children 'knew damn well they shouldn't behave like that'. Consequently an 'open door' arrangement was begun. From 8.40 a.m. children and their parents could come into the classroom and children were encouraged to get on with quiet activities. Registration was at 8.55 a.m. Staff found this started the day in a calm way. It avoided 60 children arriving at one time and all trying to use a small cloakroom. Other advantages were that it cut down the 'gate committee'– the head's term for the sometimes noisy parents that tended to form each morning – and it allowed parents and teachers to meet in a relaxed and usually one to one fashion.

There was a similar arrangement at another school. The head was insistent that children should transfer straight from home to school each morning. She was all too aware of her own school days when children were left at the gate and had to hang about in the cold in the playground. There was a flexible start time with children and parents 'drifting' in between 8.45 and 8.55. As at the school discussed first in this section, one advantage of this arrangement was reported to be that staff and parents could meet individually. The head said that at meetings teachers from other schools would say, 'don't they all come in at once – at 8.45?' The head's answer to them was that they do, at first, but not after a while. Again, children on arrival in the classroom were encouraged to continue work, painting and so on.

Staff at a junior school also reported that a collection of parents at the school gate before school could be a problem. 'They talk and moan very loudly!' So the head and deputy head stationed themselves outside the school at the front and back 'as a presence'. Like the other two schools above they also instigated a rolling start to school from 8.50 a.m. and found that the slower, more gradual input of children into the school stopped pushing and shoving and was a great improvement.

Coming in to school, lining up and queuing

We saw in Chapter 2 that difficulties in playground behaviour could arise particularly during transition times when children were coming and going from school and playground, e.g. when queuing up after the end of playtime before coming into school and when rushing back to school in response to loud bells or whistles.

In contrast to the usual arrangement of auditory signal and collecting as a group before entering school, several schools that I visited tried alternative arrangements that had in common an attempt to make entry into school unhurried and relaxed – the belief being that this would help get classroom activities off in similar fashion.

One head said that children in her school used to line up after playtime, but she found that was when pushing and shoving tended to take place. She asked herself and her staff: 'What's lining up for?' So now there were no bells to signal the end of playtime; the end of playtime was communicated from child to child – by word of mouth as it were. In consequence children 'drift in and it cuts out the pushing and shoving, and some of the rushing. It rarely happens that one gets left outside!' Instead of queuing, children went straight into their classrooms.

A first school in the same LEA had a similar approach. Instead of a bell to end playtime, this school had a series of cards to signal that playtime was over. The head said this meant they did not get a surge of children and coming in was less abrasive. 'They filter out and they filter in. And don't get clustered.' Staff in an infant school also preferred to do away with loud signals like bells and whistles, preferring instead that children collected around their teachers who had gone into the playground.

We saw in Chapter 2 the measures taken in one school to alter physically the school building to make entry into school as smooth as possible. In addition, clear rules were devised that would leave no one in any doubt about what to do when coming into school. This contrasts with the approaches that have just been described where an attempt was made to relax a rigid type of arrangement. This difference of approach between schools was clearly highlighted for me as a result of visits to two nearby schools in London. In one, the acting head said: 'you must have rules. The school is physically difficult.' The school is a large, imposing building of three floors, and there are two parallel and large staircases that had been a constant setting for squabbles and misbehaviour (as was seen in Chapter 2). In order to take pressure off the staircases there were clear rules about which to use, and infant and juniors were timetabled to go out at different times. Children also lined up after playtime. In the nearby junior school, built to a similar design, it was also found that staircases could be flashpoint areas. Under the previous head, the children had had to come in from play through a certain staircase, and were punished if they got it wrong. In the current system children could come in whichever way they liked. The acting head said: 'there are no problems. The more rules, the harder the task for supervision. Keep rules as few as possible. We always used to line up after break. They spent hours lining up! Now children don't have to line up. After break now a "Please go in" card is held up and they all come in.'

The fact that both schools seemed now happy with their arrangements for coming in from play, indicates the difficulty one faces in arriving at general suggestions for improvements. It is perhaps not so much the specific arrangement that is important – in any case staff will have to act in terms of their particular school building and problems that have arisen – so much as the process of highlighting and taking action. This process can help give clarity of purpose to supervisors, and can make the children clear about what is expected of them – both factors helpful in smoothing behaviour at transition times.

Ways of improving the quality of play

In Chapter 2 we saw that some teaching staff were concerned at what was seen as the often low level of play in the playground, and the excessive amount of fighting and squabbling. In many schools children put on coats, go out of the school doors and the rest is up to them. For whatever reason – boredom, over-crowding have been mentioned as causes – there is cause for concern about what goes on in the playground. What can be done to improve behaviour? In this section we go beyond previous sections in this chapter in order to consider specific ways of giving children direction and ideas for outside play.

Outside equipment

If children are misbehaving or behaving in a desultory way in the playground, it may well be because they have nothing to occupy them. An obvious strategy is to give them materials and equipment which they can play with. (Permanent outside equipment is considered in Chapter 5.) Staff in schools are sometimes reluctant to do this because of the effort needed to organize distribution and collection, as well as obtaining materials in the first place and worries about losing them. These problems are real ones. Staff in one inner city infant school used to let out into the playground small apparatus like bats and balls, but found so many problems with fighting over possession, and losing balls over school walls into back-gardens, that a ban now operated on taking any equipment or toys out.

It is therefore understandable if schools show some reluctance in letting out equipment into the playground. But the experience of some staff is that it is manageable and that children enjoy it. In a junior school in North London equipment like hoops and skipping ropes was bought, as well as £50 spent on notebooks, to be taken out into the playground. Some equipment was lost but the staff accepted that this was inevitable. Staff at a middle school were also worried about squabbling, fighting and bullying in the playground and decided that children's behaviour was affected by boredom and lack of space. They therefore organized a system of loaning out PE equipment, such as skipping ropes, large balls, netball hoops, and nets. This was done at the beginning of the morning, and children had responsibility for handing back equipment at the end of the day. It was found that children were unwilling to take out equipment when cold and so the system only operated during the warmer months. It was the head's view that the system when in operation made a marked contribution to creative play. A PE adviser had been impressed enough to make a video of playground activities.

Teaching games

We saw in Chapter 2 that it was the view of some staff that children did not know how to play cooperatively with each other – certainly that they did not know many traditional games and rhymes. A direct response, taken by staff in some schools, is therefore to introduce children to games and rhymes that can be played in the playground. There is support from research for this tactic. An experimental study in the USA found that organized games for children in the playground significantly reduced the number of inappropriate and aggressive incidents (Murphy, Hutchinson, and Bailey, 1983).

In Chapter 2 we looked at the depressing account of children's outside play from a deputy head. It was decided in this school that children needed to be taught games and activities. So, for three weeks in the summer term, the children were shown games. This was done in school, during school time, and the hope was that games would be transferred to the playground. The deputy head said that it was surprisingly difficult to think up games. Her starting point was to 'dig from my own past'! She remembered the street games she used to play; games with balls, beanbags and even socks, and chasing games. She also went to the County Museum and studied a book there on Victorian games. She found interesting skipping games, and games that used small balls and string.

A good place to introduce games is during assembly; it is a time when all children are together and can highlight the importance of what happens in the playground for the whole school. Another way of introducing games is in singing and music periods. Children could be taught songs that 'we can sing in the playground'. This was the strategy of the rural Northampton primary school, referred to earlier in this chapter, as part of a general attempt to improve the quality of playground activities. They also had a children's notice board with ideas for indoor and outdoor play. In an urban infant school teachers showed children different games and in PE time they were taught circle games. Another school, as part of a sponsored skip for the Heart Foundation, supplied skipping ropes in the playground, and children were taught accompanying rhymes.

The Coombes infant school in Arborfield, Berkshire, is justly well known for the pioneering work in creating a challenging and exciting outside area, and this is described in Chapter 6. One feature of the playground, that it is appropriate to mention at this point, is the separate area devoted solely to skipping. On the school walls, that acted as one border to the area, were painted rhymes to accompany skipping, and illustrations. It is likely that children will at times need to be reminded of the use of such a display.

Examples of games that could be played during wet playtime can be found in Cotler (1980).

One teacher has written about her collection of material from children about games they knew. They were classified under the headings of claps, dips, singing games, circle games, line games, ball games, skipping games and others (Palmer, 1975). A festival was held for four schools. The children performed their games and songs and apparently took lively, and critical, interest in each other's performance. Some interesting regional differences were evident, as well as much skill, inventiveness and humour. The teacher concludes: 'The rhythms of rhymes and songs are lively but regular; the structures and shape of games are simple and clear. Repetition and clarity, however, do not preclude variety and inventiveness throughout the repertoire. If children respect clarity of form in their traditional art, will they not also favour it in creative studies in school?'

As stated in Chapter 1, there has been little research on playtime, and so little material of this nature from which teachers might draw ideas for playground activities. There have been published some packs that may well prove useful. It is not easy to get an overall picture of this material and it may well be that there are other useful documents available. The following are a few I know have been found useful: Community Service Volunteers (1980), National Playing Fields Association (1983), Orlick (1979).

For some schools, especially in inner cities, with high percentages of children from ethnic minorities, the introduction of traditional games and rhymes raises interesting possibilities. Some staff felt unsure about the kinds of games children, for example of South Asian descent, might play at home. Some thought there were no recognizable differences to the play of white children, both being heavily influenced by television, comics and videos. This is an area about which there appears to be little systematic evidence.

What is clear is that teachers would welcome advice about non-Western games and rhymes, that would help reflect the multicultural nature of their schools and the country. Such games could be introduced not only as resource for playtime, but also as a way of fostering insights into non-Western cultures. Interestingly, some writers have shown some striking similarities in children's games in different countries, for example, in England and France (Roberts, 1979) and Britain, Nigeria and Uganda (Durojaiye, 1977). Staff might find useful the paper by Nickell and Kennedy (1987), which describes games from countries throughout the world. Also, an article called 'A World of Games' in *Child Education* (May, 1987) describes some non-competitive games from countries of the world (e.g. Iran and Cameroon).

The role of adults in children's play

Given the picture that has been painted about the quality of outside play, it seems justified to teach and encourage traditional games and rhymes. Yet it might be argued that it is wrong for adults to impose their ideas on children when the whole point of playtime is that it allows children time away from adult control and direction. This point was expressed strongly by the Opies.

> In the past, traditional games were thought to be dying out, few people cared, and the games continued to flourish. In the present day we assume children to have lost the ability to entertain

themselves, we become concerned, and are liable, by our concern, to make what is not true a reality. In the long run, nothing extinguishes self-organized play more effectively than does action to promote it (1969, p.16).

Clearly, the role staff play in children's outside play is a delicate one. Too strong an influence, as the Opies maintain, may take away children's initiative and fun. On the other hand, too little direction may simply perpetuate an absence of traditional and cooperative games, and some of the behavioural difficulties in the playground that have been described in Chapter 2. How can this dilemma be resolved?

If it is the case that children are not passing on games and rhymes to each other – at least not games that would be recognized by the Opies – then it seems clear that they will have to be introduced to them somehow. Whether or not this represents an imposition on the children will depend to a large extent on how it is introduced. There is surely room here for a balanced approach, within which, for example, games are presented as possibilities for the playground, along the lines of 'games you might enjoy playing'. The bottom line is that children must enjoy the games, because otherwise they will surely drop out of use. Staff need to have awareness of what happens in the playground, and to show children that they are genuinely interested in what games children play. It is difficult to see how encouragement of this kind can be an imposition.

Discussions with teachers, sensitive to this dilemma, indicate that adults can play a necessary and important role as facilitators of children's outside play. Perhaps in a society where children do not play out in the streets, and cannot learn games from other children, and where images from the media are so influential, the handing down of games needs the active intervention of adults. Adults can be 'catalysts' in children's play. In any case, it was the experience of several teachers that once children were given an idea, far from becoming statically reproduced or dropped, it was taken up and soon changed and adapted in lively ways.

It is also the experience of staff that games will wane and drop out of use. To some extent this is part of a natural and seasonal cycle of fashion in playground activity, that is bound to take place. But it can also mean that children at times could profit from being reminded of games, and helped to try out new ones.

Involving children in decisions about the playground

Perhaps the best way of achieving a balance between teacher direction of activities, and allowing a completely free hand to children, is an approach that seeks to involve children in playground activity. It seemed to me that the most successful and imaginative use of playgrounds comes when staff work to get children thinking about, and involved in, what they do and don't like about the playground, and what use they might make of it. Published ideas about games and activities are of help, but there can be no better way of improving the quality of behaviour than initiatives that come from within schools. In this section, I describe the way staff in two schools have gone about involving children in the playground. I am sure that staff in the schools concerned would in all modesty not claim to have solved all or many of the problems arising at playtime. Moreover, there are unlikely to be general routes to success, because approaches adapted must have as their starting point the particular concerns about playtime arising out of the characteristics of individual schools. None the less, they seemed to me to offer insights into ways of involving children in the playground.

'The playground project'

In Chapter 2 we looked at the anti-social behaviour arising at playtime in a junior school in West Sussex. It was said there that an experienced teacher was assigned to the top junior class that was the source of much of the problems. We now look at the way she went about improving matters.

Her first step as we saw was to ask herself how she could most effectively improve their behaviour. Their problem behaviour showed itself in the playground, and may have been caused by it, and so that was where she started. She reasoned that simply containing behaviour was not enough; she had to engage with the children in a dialogue about their feelings toward the playground and school, and work together with them toward new ways of looking at the playground. 'I wanted to get them involved, motivated and responsive.' She started by first getting the children to 'brainstorm, debate, discuss, argue and explain their feelings about the playground'. It became very apparent that the main problem was that they were bored – 'there was nothing to do because there was nothing you were allowed to do'. As we have seen, she was also concerned about how much this contrasted with the challenges and interest provided within school.

Her approach was therefore to start a major cross-curricular project on playtime. Apart from the need to improve behaviour at playtime, there was another reason why this seemed a good choice of project: 'I knew they would all be able to contribute because it was their territory and they were the knowledgeable experts.' The class began ignoring bells and continued working when it was not convenient or appropriate to stop, going out to the playground as a class when it suited them, or perhaps not at all. This meant that when they did go out the teacher went with them. It was hard work, because she aimed not just to supervise, but to learn from the experts. 'I was always asked to participate and became a regular part of their games (tag, bulldog) and dance routines (for current pop records).' Skipping for large groups and with long ropes became popular with most of the class.

They discussed differences between their own games and those organized by teachers during PE lessons. 'They decided there were good and bad points in both.' So she challenged them to devise games for the playground (on paper), and to then chalk them out on the playground surface and try to play them. One feature of the markings was that they could involve number symbols. 'They refined and modified their designs with their experiences and eventually came up with markings and games that were far more open to a variety of interpretations than their original highly prescriptive designs.' This work was done in small groups. They later played on other group's markings, first learning the original game, but then interpreting it in their own way. the next step was to paint the markings onto the playground as permanent features.

The class also devised a competitive team game. The children's brief was that it had to have two teams and had to involve everyone all the time. The invented game comprised ball hitting, scoring runs and fielding. 'It's fast, best played by about 8-10 a side and involves elements of cricket, basketball, American football. . . . It started off with very involved and complex rules, and although still very sophisticated, it has become refined through negotiation, trial and error to its present state, and is very popular. We call it the Crazy Game because it is!'

As part of the project, children also spent the term designing and building working models of playground apparatus that could be used in parks and recreational area. The children were asked to cater for both able-bodied and disabled children. A roundabout was designed with the interests and safety of all children in mind, and included pull-up ramps that became walls for a wheelchair space on board. Swings were designed that incorporated traditional seats, chairs for toddlers and barrel or 'lolling' seats for disabled children who could not climb on to, or balance on, the swing. An adventure frame was designed that included low monkey swing bars over soft crash areas, or over trolley tracks, that could be moved along by arm or leg power (as in bridge tunnel walkers on canal barges). Many designs included spaces, cut-outs or tactile experiences for blind or partially sighted children, or children with restricted hearing.

It can be seen that the playground project involved children in a set of exercises that served to get them thinking, in fundamental ways, about the playground. It covered mathematics, craft, design and technology, and much more. Clearly parts of the work extended beyond what would ever see the light of day. It is also difficult to evaluate in any systematic way what effect this work had on playground behaviour. But it is easy to see how valuable the project must have been for the children. The teacher, though undoubtedly talented, was really applying an imaginative approach to the playground, in much the same way as she did to work in the classroom. There is so much to admire in project work in primary schools – if only the imagination of teachers and children in schools could be turned deliberately on the playground more often.

Another feature of the project was that it approached the playground from several points of view. Individually each strand was interesting, but when put together they could be a powerful force for change in children's thinking about the playground. It is this teacher's view that it should also be accompanied by a change in the views of teaching and ancillary staff in the playground. That is, the large playground and field at this school were largely a wasted resource, to some extent because breaktime was centred on the needs of staff more than children. While staff are entitled to as much consideration as the children, there are alternatives to the traditional entrenched approach to playtime. For this teacher, part of an alternative approach was the breaking down of barriers between classroom and playground. 'As a school we have demystified boundaries between school and home, but we have yet to recognize the barriers between pupil and teacher cultures.' It was the cause of frustration to her that her colleagues seemed reluctant to extend the schools' beliefs about learning beyond the barriers of the school, which would include a fundamental examination of the playground and what might be done there.

The children's council

In a junior school in Brent I came across another exciting, but very different, approach to involving children in decisions about the playground.

It began as part of the development of an equal opportunities policy for the school. It was quickly realized, however, that dealing with behaviour in classroom and school, for example the tendency of boys to push in and dominate, was only part of the problem, because differences and inequalities occurred in the playground. As in many schools, for example, football tended to dominate playground space, and this meant that the playground was dominated by boys, usually the stronger more outspoken ones.

The staff discussed how all children might have their say about the playground, and for this purpose set up a 'children's council'. Each week, first thing on Thursday morning, each class would hold discussions. Each class elected two representatives, and the sessions would be chaired by one, while the other took down notes of what was said – in a sense took the minutes. There was some direction from the teacher in the initial selection of reps, so that a boy and girl were elected, and also, if possible, children of different ages (classes were vertically grouped, with first and second year together and third and fourth together). There was also some teacher help, especially with the younger classes, in establishing some basic rules, for example, that only one person could speak at a time, and that everyone's views should be listened to, and not denigrated, no matter how silly they might seem. But the intention was for teachers to stand back and as far as possible let the children run the discussions.

Later on the same day the two elected representatives from each class would then meet the head and bring up points raised in the class discussions. The topics discussed were not confined to playtime but it was found that many of the topics raised concerned that part of the school day – an indication of its important place in the children's perceptions of the school. Moreover, at one point during the term, the school was putting together a submission to Brent LEA for Urban Programme Funds (see Chapter 5), and children's views on the playground environment were encouraged in order to feed into this proposal.

The head said that there were some 'weird and wild ideas' voiced at the meetings with her, but that by and large most concerns were sensible and showed that the children had considered problems in a thoughtful way. Many of the comments were of the form: 'why don't you do this about so and so?' The head would then try to get them to think about the consequences of such an action. For example, a clear view expressed was for football to be banned. (One consequence of a relatively 'democratic' selection of reps was that the banning of football was able to come from the children on to the agenda at all. Without such a structure the outspoken and powerful boys might quite likely have kept such a subversive notion at bay.) But the head asked them to consider what would take its place. Such was the council's strength of feeling, a compromise was reached and football was confined to a certain area. This, however, did not work because the area became too crowded and there were arguments over who should play. During the current term, therefore, the school had introduced a new arrangement – football was only to be played with tennis balls and between teams of up to three-a-side.

There was in the school a lot of play in the playground with marbles. Many of the children's worries concerned arguments over marbles and much of the head's time was spent sorting out problems that arose because of it. The head therefore encouraged the reps to get the children to make rules, before they started to play, so that it would be clear how to settle disputes.

Another request from the children was for a climbing frame for the playground. The head agreed it would be a good idea, and got them to consider the safety and financial consequences. The head was amused that one child in the council could now be relied on to take the role she was accustomed to playing. In response to proposals from his fellow reps, he would say, 'but have we got the money?'

Many of their ideas on improving the playground were included in the submission to Brent LEA. They asked for a quiet area and seating, for those who did not want to engage in boisterous games, a garden area, and a high fence to shield the area devoted to ball games. One of their more extravagant ideas was for fountains 'like those in Trafalgar Square'! It was the head's experience that the children had little or no appreciation of the cost of their proposals. Guesses were vague and inaccurate. They asked tentatively if the proposals would be as much as £100? (To be fair, the head also said that the staff themselves had greatly underestimated the cost of their proposals.)

So what were the staff's conclusions about the children's council? First of all a lot of children now felt confident about stepping in during playground disputes. The head was quick to point out that problems still arose in the playground, but that there were now well-aired rules, which the children had a hand in devising, and which they had a commitment to upholding, and so there was a firmer foundation for acceptable playground behaviour.

A second benefit was that it encouraged children to think for themselves, and moreover to think realistically about the consequences of decisions. But a third, and for the head most gratifying, consequence was for the development of a moral dimension to the children's contributions. For example, one request from the reps was for a particularly troublesome boy to be banned from the playground. At first the children wanted the child banned forever but one child pointed out that that would not do the offending child any good because if he did not go into the playground how would he then learn how to play? As a result of this intervention, a decision was taken to ban the child for two weeks in the first instance. Another suggestion – in view of the domination of boys in the playground area reserved for ball games – was that in the morning only girls should be able to use the area and in the afternoon boys would get a turn. However, there was a clear body of opinion from the children that this would be wrong because girls and boys should learn to play together. The head said that these kinds of opinions showed courage, in the sense that expression of a willingness, even a wish, to play with the opposite sex would previously have been ridiculed by peers. The council had therefore created an atmosphere which allowed children to say more honestly what they felt.

This is a benefit over and above the fundamental creation of a channel through which children can express their views. In this context it is relevant to note the work I saw in schools which attempted to get children to write out or draw, for example, their ideas for improving the playground, or designing their 'ideal' playground. This kind of work can lead to interesting results. One limitation with it, however, is that it may not bring children into a real dialogue with teachers about the playground. Even when mounted on walls for display such work is still at a distance from staff, as it were, and not something entered into discussion or playing a big part in decisions taken. This is one reason why the idea of the children's council seems to me so attractive. It creates conditions through which the imagination and feelings of children can find expression, and which directly confronts teachers into reactions and dialogue. And, as we have seen, it can directly involve children in the creation and maintenance of playground rules.

4
Lunchtime: Problems and Improvements

In the vast majority of primary and secondary schools in Britain there are up to three breaks in the school day: in the morning, in the afternoon and at lunchtime. Time after time one hears the same judgement: most problems in the playground occur at lunchtime. Moreover, because of recent changes, there are reasons for thinking the situation is getting worse, and that heads in particular are under increasing strain. It is the aim of this chapter to show the nature and severity of these problems, and to argue that action must be taken to improve things.

Why do most problems occur at lunchtime? Perhaps the first and most obvious reason is because it is far longer than either the morning and afternoon breaks – usually more than twice as long, in fact, than both put together. There are likely to be more problems therefore in proportion to its length. In addition, children can become tired and cold after so long a time outside, and, as we saw in Chapter 2, there is then more chance of petty or accidental knocks resulting in conflict.

Lunchtime supervision

But this is not the only difference. There is also a difference in the supervision provided for children. In recent years it has undergone a major, and it seems irreversible, change. It was during the Second

World War that children started to stay at schools at lunchtime. Since then teachers have supervised at lunchtime, or at least been around the school, in the classroom, taking clubs and so on, and were a calming influence on the children. Even if in the staffroom, they were prepared to be on call.

This has now all changed. The change probably in fact dates back to 1960s when the teaching unions began to get concerned about what was seen as an increasing requirement to do lunchtime duty. But events took a drastic turn during the recent industrial action, when many teachers absented themselves from lunchtime duties, as they were entitled to do. Many of the clubs and other activities, that depended on teachers' goodwill, now floundered.

The 1987 School Teachers' Pay and Conditions Document then formally set out teachers' duties, and quantified them in terms of 'working time' (DES, 1987). Whereas activities with children during lunchbreaks and after school once occurred because of teachers' goodwill and because of tradition, now teachers have fallen in with the spirit of the new conditions, and take the lunchbreak many feel they need and are entitled to. And there is a strong case for the benefits of a mid-day break; continuous contact with children is very demanding.

Of course this varies between schools, and in some teachers will have more contact with children at lunchtime. There is likely to be contact, for example, as teachers prepare for the afternoon, fetch coffee, eat their lunch and so on. Teachers in some authorities are also accepting payments to supervise at lunchtime. In some schools I visited clubs were beginning to return. But for the most part teachers do not seem to play the active part in lunchtime supervision that they once did.

So, if teachers do not now supervise at lunchtime, who does? In most schools this is effectively in the hands of ancillary staff, employed for that purpose. During the teachers' industrial action the problem of supervision at lunchtime in some schools reached crisis point, and in order to stop schools closing, extra money was allocated to take on more supervisory staff. So the government, at that time at least, recognized the need to provide alternative arrangements for lunchtime supervision, and supervision at lunchtime by ancillary staff is now firmly established.

Different LEAs have different arrangements, but commonly a school will have a number of mid-day supervisors, in proportion to the size of school and, in some LEAs, in relation to such factors as the layout of the school and positioning of playgrounds. The official term given to supervisors varies between LEAs. For example, in some they are called 'mid-day assistants' (MDAs), in others 'school meal supervisory assistants' (SMSAs). In the School Teachers' Pay and Conditions Document, 1987, they are called 'mid-day supervisors'. It was not uncommon for heads to have to think hard to remember the official nomenclature. Most refer to them as 'dinner ladies'. They are responsible to the head, though in some authorities this is mediated through the appointment of senior supervisors. Arrangements for the appointment of supervisors again vary; in some schools, dinner supervisors will be known to heads because their own children are, or have been, at the school, and in some authorities, their names may be supplied to schools by the authority itself. They are often appointed after no more than an informal chat with the head of school. Apart from a medical, no formal qualifications or experience are required. They are appointed for the duration of the lunchbreak. Their pay again varies; as an example, in Ealing LEA senior supervisors are paid £5.50 a session. Their responsibilities will include supervision of the children in the dining hall and in the playground.

In some schools, these arrangements can work well, and on most days, in most schools, life in the dining hall and in the playground probably proceeds without major mishaps. In some schools, one will hear heads speak warmly about a particular supervisor. One head said: 'I've got an older lady who is very astute and intelligent. She takes a lead, otherwise you get factions.' In a similar vein another head said: 'My senior SMSA is very reliable. She's a grandmother. The children respect her. She's not a barker or a Sergeant Major – really homely but with firm standards.' And another head spoke about the contrast between what he considered to be a model supervisor and her younger colleagues.

> She's the wife of the school caretaker, and a grandmother. She understands and cares for children in a way younger supervisors don't seem to. She has a collection of 'goodies' in a bag that children can play with. She takes children in hand if they are upset, or loners. She'll talk to them, take them around with her, get them involved in an activity and then withdraw. She gets games going. Everything she does has a purpose. She doesn't see

her job as sentry duty. She deals with problems herself. Only once has she brought a child to me. She eliminates problems before they arise. She's able to deal with children in an involved yet even-handed way – a good listener and a good organizer.

It is interesting to note the qualities in supervisors that heads feel are important – and we shall return to this later in the chapter. It is also important to acknowledge the contribution – largely unsung – that such people make to school life. Schools are lucky to have them. But it is also important to say that they are probably not common, and that effective supervisors with the skills just described are more the result of good fortune than the product of any policy or training.

If there has been unanimous agreement on one thing during my visits to schools it is that the quality of supervision provided at lunchtime is not as good as that provided during the rest of the school day, including that provided by teachers in the playground during the other two breaks. The following quote from a head summarizes many of the points made by other teachers:

I'm worried at the children's attitudes to them. As much as I say to the children that they should treat dinner staff as members of staff, they don't respect them. It's because they haven't got the child management skills and sometimes make foolish decisions and shout at them [the children]. And the biggest problem – they don't anticipate trouble. Only two of them see conflicts coming. Others intervene when crisis occurs. One intelligent boy worked out the system. He knew he should tell dinner staff if something had happened but he knew he would have to in the end tell one of the teachers, so he found it easier to say he wanted to go to the toilet, and go up to see me. So I'm concerned and the parents are concerned. Very often in discussion with parents playground behaviour comes up.

It is worth looking in more detail at views about supervision provided by supervisors. One feature, mentioned by the head just quoted, is the different way children are seen to react to supervisors and teachers. Here are quotes from other heads on the same subject:

Children treat dinner ladies in a way they never would teachers. They see them as third rate people.

> It is difficult to get children to see SMSAs as teachers and difficult to get SMSAs to see children as teachers do.

> Children have a lack of respect for dinner ladies.

> Dinner ladies haven't got the authority we have and children know it.

> Children are verbally abusive to dinner ladies. They don't see them as authority. They lip them in a way they never would teachers.

Some heads felt that the children's attitudes were abetted by the attitudes of some parents. For example, one head heard a mother say to her child: 'You don't have to take any notice of her, she's only a mid-day.' Some parents view the lunchtime supervisor as just another mother, and see their post as having low prestige.

Another common observation was that lunchtime supervisors do not have skills of managing children. For example, they try to control children with 'empty' threats that they do not (and in some cases should not be allowed to) follow through, they do not anticipate trouble but instead respond aggressively after it has occurred, and they do not respond adequately to children's worries:

> They haven't got the same control as teachers.

> Their management skills are low. They haven't got presence. Even I can't see them in the playground.

> SMSAs can punish but the follow up is missing.

> Children come to me upset at lunchtime. I say, did you see a dinner lady. They say she told me to go away and play.

> At lunchtime the framework is slacker. There's less sense of clear discipline.

One must bear in mind that these are comments by teaching staff, and it would require more detailed study – both observational and of supervisors' views – to be sure about their accuracy. But heads are uniquely placed to have direct experience of the consequences of the supervision provided, and can compare it with that provided by teachers. The quality of supervision may not be the main cause of problems in the playground, but the quality of play is bound to be affected by it.

There were also worries about the way supervisors tended to behave in heavy-handed way toward children.

> They have a strange way of talking. They always see things in black or white. They can't modify punishment to the child. Can't treat them as individuals.

> They shout to get a response. They don't know how to deal with fighting – they pick on a child with a bad reputation.

> One dinner lady had totally the wrong attitude – she marched them up and down. A disciplinarian. She felt her job was getting them all quiet.

> They mete out punishment. They can be heavy-handed.

We can see here, and we saw in Chapter 2, that there were worries in some schools about the even-handedness of supervisors in their dealings with children, for example in the way that some supervisors appeared too quick to accuse children who already had a bad reputation, and how this could be based on presuppositions related to a child's sex or ethnic group.

Wet play

Problems of supervision at lunchtime are aggravated if the weather is bad enough to confine the children to the school building. As one head said 'if the weather is fine we can manage, but wet play is a real pain. It is very difficult for three SMSAs even with the head and deputy head to cope with whole school.' Another head said 'wet play with four dinner ladies and 200 children in the hall is absolute death'. Others complained that the allowance of supervisors was simply not enough to provide one for each class, and so it was difficult to provide adequate supervision when children went to their classrooms. And it should be remembered that lunchtime can be as much as an hour and a half long. In such circumstances many admitted getting through lunch was simply a holding operation. One head worried that videos were now shown in the hall to children as a matter of course; she felt they should be only one of several options on offer.

Employing mothers of children in school as supervisors

In one authority, which had previously supplied names to schools of potential lunchtime supervisors, a move was being made to get schools themselves to enlist supervisors, and in particular, mothers of children in school. Comments from heads in authorities where this arrangement had been in place for years suggested it could cause problems. A head of a junior and infant school after nine years' experience, said that when the next supervisor left (she had been with school for 22 years) he would not appoint as lunchtime supervisors mothers of children in the school. His experience was that it was difficult for their children to cope –'even the most placid of children expect favours'. And he said he had yet to find a supervisor who was not affected by having their own child in school. It was very difficult for them to distance themselves from their own children and their friends, and what they heard about other children. The head said it was vital that supervisors are seen by children to deal fairly with everyone. In his time he had seen unfairness, albeit unconscious, for example, supervisors acting on what their daughters had said, and judgements on children before they had opened their mouths. The head felt that problems in the playground were often to do with the perceptions of children about whether they would be treated fairly. If this was not their expectation, or they did not feel supervisors were responsive to their concerns, then problem behaviour was more likely to ensue. The head insisted that children go to an adult if there was a problem in the playground. But this strategy was called into question if children did not see adults in charge as fair, or the response to a child's difficulty was, for example, 'go and play'.

The head and deputy head of an infant school also referred to problems that arose because of mothers of children in the school being lunchtime supervisors. In particular they were worried about the problems supervisors – indeed all of us – have in dealing equally fairly with all children when one happens to be your own child. They pointed to the strong urge to defend your own children and their friends if in trouble, and to be affected by what you have heard through them about other children. They were also worried about the issue of confidentiality. They had, for example, recently had to deal with a difficult situation that had arisen when a supervisor was upset by the way her child had been treated by another child and so had sent her husband up to confront the head about it. Another problem was that supervisors tended to be away when their child was ill and it was difficult to get supply help.

Not all heads referred to this as a problem, or else they felt, along with one head, that it could be overcome by telling supervisors that they 'were employed to treat all children equally'.

Not blaming the mid-day supervisor

An important point needs to be made. It is not the intention here to blame problems that arise at lunchtime on dinner supervisors. Personal criticisms are not appropriate; it is the wider context which structures the employment of supervisors that must be addressed. Supervisors are simply not trained for a very difficult and demanding job. As one head said 'absolutely nothing has been done for lunchtime staff'. They are at the bottom end of the employment market – badly paid and, as we have seen, not held in high regard. The hours are limited and inconvenient for many people. Good candidates are unlikely to be attracted. It comes as no surprise to learn in schools that there were problems recruiting staff and in obtaining relief supervisors, if any were away. One head simply could not appoint a senior SMSA – current supervisors were not prepared to take on the extra responsibility for so little extra reward.

They do not get much support. While some authorities do provide courses for supervisors to attend on a voluntary basis (for example, Brent and the ILEA), most do not appear to. Opportunities within schools for support and liaison with teaching staff are also limited. Even staff in schools that made efforts to set up meetings with supervisors, and provided written guidelines for supervisors, found it was very difficult to find time when all could get together. Moreover, supervisors are rarely paid to attend such meetings. Contact with class teachers is often reduced to little more than a hurried account of an individual incident at lunchtime, given as teachers take over for the afternoon session.

If teaching staff can detect the frustrations of supervisors, then one imagines the feelings of supervisors themselves. A survey of the views of 77 dining supervisors by a group of heads in Leicestershire found that nearly two-thirds found their duties 'onerous and demanding', and only 12 per cent expressed themselves as being well satisfied. A resignation about their lot is suggested by the fact that the great majority (78 per cent) thought that little could be done to improve matters (Beaumanor Research Group, unpublished report).

Considering the conditions of employment of supervisors, perhaps it is remarkable that the service provided at lunchtime is as good as it is. Supervisors need and deserve more support. As one head said: 'It is crucial that SMSAs are trained. It is a far more difficult job than they and others realize.'

The strain on heads

Before we move on to look at what might be done to improve lunchtime supervision it is important to describe another important effect of recent changes. If lunchtime used to prosper because of the goodwill of teachers, it now depends on the goodwill of heads. Heads are faced with two competing demands. On the other hand, they have overall responsibility for the school at lunchtime, and must be concerned about issues, for example of children's safety. On the other, they are also aware that they too need a break. Officially they are 'entitled to a break of reasonable length in the course of each school day, and shall arrange for a suitable person to assume responsibility for the discharge of his [sic] functions as head teacher during that break,' (GB.DES, 1987).

But as one head said: 'Heads don't have a break. Literally you don't. I walk the building. Yesterday I ate my Ryvita at 3 o'clock. It's uncivilized. The professional organization is making little progress. Officially I'm entitled to lunchtime.' Another said: 'I've never had a dinner break in 21 years, and I resent it!' And another head said: 'I've got ulcers because I never sit down at lunch.'

The less that teachers contribute to supervision at lunchtime, the greater the burden on heads. Many are feeling the extra strain. 'It is better for teachers not having to supervise lunch, but I feel exposed. If they're at the pub on Friday I'm the only member of the teaching staff on site.' 'If, say, the inspector rings up at lunchtime I can't answer it if we're short staffed.'

There were also worries about the responsibility for children's safety. 'If a child was stabbed in a classroom at lunchtime [during wet play] I don't know where we'd stand.' 'The head and deputy head can never both be out of school [at lunchtime]. I rang up the office and asked who's in charge [at lunchtime] if the head and deputy head are out. The office didn't know.'

The position of deputy heads can also be difficult. They have to stand in for the head if he or she is away. In any case they may feel obliged to offer the head support, and in effect be on duty at lunchtime. But unlike the head they usually will then have to take a class immediately after lunch, and teach for the rest of the day.

In my experience, heads sympathize with the stand of the teachers' unions, and think it is proper for teachers to take a break away from children at lunchtime. But it is difficult to believe that the separation of heads and teachers over lunchtime supervision has helped relationships within the school. When the door closes at lunchtime on a full staffroom, it is inevitable that heads will sometimes feel isolated. And it is likely that heads will feel more isolated and pressurized in relation to the extent of problems that arise at lunchtime.

Of course, the majority of heads willingly take control of the school at lunch. Most heads have a strong sense of responsibility toward their school and children. Many are tolerant and good humoured in the face of constant interrruptions and constant calls on their time. But lunchtime at present is containable in the way it is to a large extent because these qualities are exploited. The situation is not fair and it is not professional. It can leave heads exhausted and frustrated, and this can do little to help them perform well their functions within school. That many do this, and provide leadership in ways that make schools special places to be in, is a tribute to their personal qualities. But it could be, and should be, made less difficult for them.

What can be done?

Given the problems that have been described, many might be forgiven for arguing that a lunchtime break of the length traditional in this country is not necessary. Indeed alternatives to the way the school day is currently organized, are very much under review at present, and we look at these in Chapter 6.

But it is unlikely that changes like this will be widespread, at least in the near future, and so we look here at ways existing arrangements for lunchtime – that is, supervision provided for its duration by lunchtime supervisors – might be improved.

The essential question is this: if teachers are no longer a part of the equation, how can we ensure quality of supervision at lunchtime? At the moment, for the reasons described, we do not have the best possible arrangements.

I look now at possible improvements, suggested by visits to schools. There is also the issue of general resources for lunchtime supervision. I take this up in Chapter 7.

One obvious improvement would be simply to increase the numbers of supervisors in schools. This would be helpful during wet play, when, as we have seen, there may not be enough supervisors to adequately supervise the children in their classes.

But the most important and necessary objective must be to improve the quality of supervision provided. The ways in which this might occur will be dependent on the aims staff and governors have for playtime – a point I take up in Chapter 7. But it is possible here to identify three directions for improvement. They are not mutually exclusive.

1 Involving supervisors in whole school policies

To return to a theme of Chapter 3, it makes little sense to have a policy on, or a set of rules about, behaviour and discipline at school, if this is not carried over into the playground. This is given added weight when one remembers that about a quarter of the school day will be spent at lunch or playtime (see Chapter 1). If there is not to be a separation between school and playtime, then supervisors must be very familiar with the school's policies, and, better still, have had some part in their construction. Indeed, they should be seen as having responsibility for carrying out the school's policies. We saw in Chapter 3 an example of a whole school being involved in the creation of a code of conduct for the playground. It must be the responsibility of teaching staff to acquaint supervisors with their views and policies on behaviour. If there are strong views, for example on cooperation in learning, equal opportunities, anti-racism and so on, it is useless to simply hope that supervisors will perform their function in agreement with those views, or to moan about them if they do something different; they must be better informed.

The greater involvement of supervisors will also allow parents to see clearly the key role supervisors have in implementing school policies, and also the expectation of teaching staff that the supervisor is to be respected.

2 Liaison between teaching staff and supervisors

As we have seen, while staff and supervisors do make efforts to meet and discuss school policies and children, many will agree that it is difficult to find time for this. The success of liaison at present depends on the goodwill of teaching and supervisory staff. While this is obviously essential, and in some cases liaison no doubt works well, it works by exploiting that goodwill. For example, supervisors are not paid to attend such meetings. In consequence, the frustrations of supervisors can build up, and teaching staff cannot adequately discuss school policies or the behaviour and progress of individual children. This is one reason for the clear division in many schools between the school and the playground.

One way to improve supervision at lunchtime, and at the same time to help integrate it with the classroom, is therefore to ensure that liaison between supervisors and teaching staff is more extensive, and to offer a structure within which such meetings are encouraged and given direction.

Support could come from the LEA. This could be financial – for example, to provide funds for meetings to take place – and also in terms of direction and support for meetings. Some LEAs have offered assistance of these kinds. And there are no doubt other kinds of support that I have not heard about. But there is also little doubt that more could be done. I return below to the subject of support with training of lunchtime supervisors.

A change of arrangements within schools can help, as the experience of staff in one infant school highlights. Several years ago staff were worried by the length of the lunch break – from 12 to 1.30 p.m. In particular it was found that the worst traumas occurred in the last minutes of the lunch break. 'When Kenneth Baker imposed his pay and conditions we discussed how to allocate the contact hours in the school day and decided to shortern the lunchbreak by 15 minutes. However we didn't change the hours of the dinner supervisors.' All supervisors had responsibility for all children at lunchtime, but each also had a specific responsibility to children in one class. This meant for example that they supervised the washing of 'their' class's hands, and at the end of the lunch period they brought the children to the classroom. There was then a 15 minute period when both supervisor and teacher were in the classroom together with the children. The head called it a 'pastoral hand-over period'. It meant teachers could inform the supervisors about, for example, the specific problems of certain children, which would help make supervisors more sensitive to children's behaviour in the playground. And there was now time for teachers to learn about how their children had been behaving when out of their care in the playground and in the dining hall. It would also allow children to see teacher and supervisor collaborating, and to help improve integration of care. Supervisors can also see teachers' methods of dealing with children.

The head said: 'It is very important that we've done this. It's part of whole school policy. Often children can't cope with the change in authority. This helps merge the two.'

One feature of the approach in this school is the assignment of a supervisor to a particular class. Others also found this helped improve relationships between children and supervisor, and helped provide a basis for communication between supervisor and teacher. Of course this is affected by the numbers of supervisors available to schools, and may not always be possible.

3 Training of lunchtime supervisors

As we have seen, lunchtime supervisors receive little or no training. It is difficult to see how improvements can take place without more being provided. It is also a necessary step in improving the prestige and working conditions of supervisors. They have an important job to do and this needs to be acknowledged and supported far more than at present.

What would such training look like? During discussions with staff in schools this was a question around which much was said and it led me to the identification of four main areas that would need to be covered.

Child development

It is important for supervisors to have some knowledge of child development and learning, and in particular the role and value of play in the developmental process. This would help supervisors place children's playground experience in the context of school life in general, and also help them encourage play. It is of little use complaining that supervisors do not offer children constructive suggestions for cooperative play, when it may be because supervisors do not share teachers often implicitly held assumptions about child development, acquired during training and at school.

It would not be difficult to provide an introduction to the value of imaginative play, cooperative and singing games, story telling, number games and oral communication, along with examples of practice.

More specifically, it would also be helpful to provide guidance on learning difficulties and special educational needs.

Strategies for the management of children

Supervisors are expected to look after the needs of children but, as we have seen, they do not have the same skills in managing children that teachers have. Again, it is pointless criticizing supervisors for not having skills that teachers acquire through training and from other teachers. Some main strategies could be made explicit for supervisors. To pick up on skills identified as important by heads: there could be emphasis on anticipation and planning rather than reaction to misbehaviour, the use of a consistent set of sanctions that can be carried out, an emphasis on positive reinforcement, strategies for dealing with children in large groups, the importance of being seen to be fair and considerate, and strategies for 'conflict resolution'. Some skill in these areas would do more than make supervision in the playground and dining hall more effective; it would help to build up supervisors' confidence and prestige.

Knowledge of LEA and school policies

As we have seen, in order to provide consistency of purpose throughout the school day, it is also important that supervisors have knowledge of, and involvement in, school policies. But schools are part of, and are influenced by, policies of their LEA, and part of supervisors' training should be basic familiarization with the LEA policies, for example in such matters as equal opportunities and anti-racism. Even with the best will in the world, racism and sexism in society at large is going to be reflected in playgrounds, and so LEA policies have to be made explicit to supervisors. As shown above, it is during the long lunch break when most extreme forms of unacceptable behaviour can occur and supervisors need to be shown ways of responding in accord with LEA and school policies. This is a difficult and complex area, that can arouse misrepresentation and hostility, as the recent press response to leaks from the inquiry into the Manchester playground murder has illustrated. People can be easily put off. I met one supervisor who had been upset by her experience of a course on anti-racism provided by her LEA, which she saw as promoting the interests of black over white children. But it is no answer simply to leave supervisors in ignorance of these issues, and the way LEA and teaching staff view them. Clearly any training in this area will require sensitivity and tact. But it should be done. Supervisors' relations with children, and their contribution to school life, should benefit.

Health and safety

The most basic responsibility of lunchtime supervision is to ensure the safety and well-being of children. Schools vary in their arrangements for such matters as fire drills, procedures for dealing with accidents and illness, and so do guidelines to supervisors. Some offer clear instructions, perhaps at an induction meeting, while others are less explicit. The situation is some schools is less than satisfactory. Several heads told me that there was no legal requirement for any member of staff to have a first-aid qualification. As one said, 'parents would be horrified if they knew'. Another head recounted the panic that followed a case of severe bleeding.

It would be a fairly straightforward matter to include basic procedures in the training package. It could include action to be taken in the case of accidents and emergencies.

How could training be best carried out? There are clearly going to be many other priorities for funds, and the amounts of money available are likely to be limited. Faced with this, it is understandable that LEAs have not provided money for what is not seen a high profile need. I hope that the arguments presented in this chapter have done enough to show that this attitude is short sighted. In any case, in the absence of any funding, even small amounts could do much to help. And it would be possible to provide useful kinds of training that should not prove too expensive.

Training could take at least two forms. The first would be an LEA initiative, which would provide training for supervisors out of schools. For example, courses of say three weeks length could be provided, run by advisory staff, perhaps on the model of playleader courses. The course would aim to cover the four areas described above. A main component would be strategies for dealing with playground incidents, perhaps using video recordings of playtimes. A heavy dose of theory is unlikely to be effective or acceptable, and the course should aim to provide practical help, structured around clear guidelines.

Secondly, there could also be a school-based initiative, that could include time for heads and deputy heads to spend with supervisors, showing them strategies and offering advice, again structured around clear guidelines. There will be aspects of a supervisors' job that are bound to be tied to a particular school – for example, specific characteristics of the playground, dinner arrangements and children may all affect the kind of supervision provided – and so general packages are likely to be of limited use. There is likely to be no better way of learning ways of managing children, and of the way staff view behaviour and conduct, than to learn directly from senior staff in schools. It might, incidentally, serve to inform teaching staff more directly about problems that arise at lunchtime and serve to clarify and sharpen a school's approach to such matters.

One head had given this matter a good deal of thought. She particularly wanted to hold sessions – perhaps a whole lunch break – when teaching and ancillary staff could meet and clarify and develop procedured for effective supervision. It might also be possible to invite a speaker to the school, with particular experience in this field.

There is another useful resource that would require only a modest investment. It would be possible to make a video recording that covered the four main areas above, again illustrated with practical advice and incidents in the playground and dining hall. If the alternative is no training at all, then the viewing of such a film, with discussion afterwards with teaching staff, should be an essential requirement for the post of supervisor. It could be compulsory in the same way that a medical must be passed. It could be produced by advisory staff in the LEA.

5
The Playground Environment

One thing that strikes anyone who visits a number of schools is the enormous range of shapes and sizes of playgrounds. Some schools can have large areas, made up of a hard covered area, a field, and perhaps woodland and shrub, while other schools, often in cities, can have little more than a small, asphalt covered patch, enclosed between school and external walls. One is impressed by how arbitrary this variation is, yet how much it must affect what goes on in the playground.

Despite this variation, there is much similarity in the use that is made of playgrounds. The playground described in Chapter 1 is probably typical of many. As an environment for children's play it is often barren and visually depressing, with harsh lines and hard surfaces, and with little or no equipment. There may be a few faded game markings on the surface for hopscotch and other games, and perhaps markings, such as targets, on a wall, but very little else on which children can focus. Grassed areas may seem on a summer's day to be a valuable extension to the playground, but many are often too muddy to be used for most of the school year. Such an environment has little to offer children and makes no contribution to their education. The insights and achievements of the 'adventure playground' movement, for example, about the value of flexible, open-ended equipment, seem not to have had a great effect on school playgrounds.

Many of the changes to playground life that have been described in other chapters, though important contributions, are dealing with the symptoms of a barren playground. For example, we have seen how involving children in the playground might help enhance the quality of their play, and we have looked at possible improvements to supervision and arrangements for playtime. Some have also gone to great lengths to alter the outside of the school in order to reduce hazards and flashpoints. Yet it could be argued that all these initiatives miss one essential point: they do not deal with the fact that the playground environment itself is uninteresting and that this may be one cause of aggressive and desultory behaviour.

One might draw a parallel with the classroom in infant schools today with those say 30 years ago. Then they might well have consisted of rows of desks and not much else except a few direct aids on the walls, like letters of the alphabet. Now, as I describe in a moment, they are often well managed and colourful resources for learning. Perhaps it is time that we applied the same kind of attention to the playground. But this will only come about with a fundamental shift in thinking about the school premises. It means thinking of the school as an environmental resource, not confined to the school building, but extending to all the premises. In this way, as we shall see, the playground can become as valuable as the classroom as a way of affecting children's learning.

In recent years there has been a growing dissatisfaction with the facilities provided for children in the playground, and there have been some interesting and important improvements. In this chapter we look at some of these. This is a large area of interest that covers many different approaches, and it is not possible here to offer a comprehensive review. The strategy will be to attempt to give an overview of some main areas; to offer, by way of illustration, some schemes of which I have had direct experience; and to refer to relevant research.

Playground game markings

Often the only aspect of a playground that is deliberately created to give some direction to children's play is the game markings on the playground surface. They can be predictable and unimaginative in design. Sometimes schools have no control over them. Staff and children in one school came back from the summer holiday to find markings on the asphalt. No one knew who had designed them, and no one explained what to do with them. More often, markings have been put down at some point in the past, and are now fading and, apart from the occasional game of hopscotch, or the short-lived flurry of interest that accompanies a game currently in fashion, can be walked over unused and unnoticed.

A way has to be found to involve children in the use of the markings in the playground. This could be done by reminding children at intervals about what is available and discussing with them the kinds of games that can be played. In a similar way to the introduction of cooperative and traditional games, this might well be done in assembly, perhaps around a discussion of what markings the playground has got, and what games might be played on them. But the most effective way of making use of playground markings is to involve children right from the start, if possible in the design, and certainly the use of playground markings. We saw in Chapter 3 one way this worked in the West Sussex school where the pupils in one top junior class, as part of a project on the playground, devised and chalked out games for the playground, around the theme of number symbols.

Another initiative started as a project within which children designed and set out on paper their ideas for markings. They also worked on rules for games with markings. An LEA adviser was then approached and spent two or three afternoons with the children, clarifying what they wanted, and scaling up the most successful of the designs. He then took on the job of transferring the drawings to the playground surface. In consultation with the borough architects, and with the free loan of equipment from the Highways Department, the markings were first chalked out and then paint was applied. The aim was to make as good a job as possible, because it was recognized that these would be permanent fixtures, and so the adviser's expertise was called for.

There were frustrations. One was that it seemed to take far longer than had originally been intended and the advisor was worried that the children might begin to lose their initial interest. He was also conscious that he might begin to be seen merely as 'the man with the machine', as the process of getting down markings dragged on, partly because of difficulties in fitting around playtimes.

But the newly laid down designs were attractive, and inviting. One design was of a rocket, divided into eleven sections with number symbols from 0 (the nose) to 10 (the base). There was a traditional hopscotch design, alongside a hopscotch on the theme of a 'haunted house', with pictures of skeletons, ghosts, spiders, and bats. Another design was of a snake-like shape with a recurring sequence of coloured squares, rectangles, triangles and circles. This, like the other designs, had rules that the children had invented – the snake, for example, was an 'elimination' game in which children landing on certain shapes had to get off, while other children continued. But, apparently, as soon as the designs were put down they created a good deal of interest among the children and there was a lot of invention of, and arguing over, rules. Children were quick to interpret the game to suit themselves. The advisory teacher was making a video of each stage of the project, and the use children made of the markings.

This is another way of involving children in a fundamental way in their play in the playground, in line with the schemes described in Chapter 3. The children in this school were given the opportunity to have some say in the design, and certainly in the rules of using, the markings, and this degree of involvement is likely to be proportional to the later interest children show in them. However, there is also likely to be benefit from reminders later on, as new children come into the school. In this respect, there was one ingredient that seemed to be lacking from the initiative just described – there was relatively little teacher involvement in the exercise. In one sense this was an advantage, in that it allowed more freedom for the children; but it is also possible that later reminders might be less than enthusiastic when none of the teachers had any part to play in their original design.

Another approach is to use game markings much more directly as an extension of classroom activities. Recently the principal of an elementary school in Kansas City in the USA has described how playtime ('recess') in her school is now called 'Play and Learn (PAL)' time (Wholf, 1984). Thirty 'graphics' relating to most subject areas and age levels adorn walls and ground. Over a two-year period teachers created the designs and professional artists transferred them. Several graphics are designed to develop vocabulary. For example, one section of the playground, with three columns of 20 words each, is called the 'magic carpet'. Children are told they are going on a magic-carpet ride. To get to land they must move around the carpet, pronouncing each word as they step on it. If they do not know a word, they 'fall off'. There is another design comprising consonant clusters. There is a circle that works by stressing the correspondence between percentages, fractions and decimals. There is a large maths race track that can be used to review a variety of number concepts, and a hopscotch with number words. The school even has 250 words, including the 50 State names, that winds its way around the outside of the playground. In this school the playground has deliberately been reconsidered in terms of an obvious educational role. Supervision has more of a teaching function. But the aim is for it to be fun and for concepts experienced in the classroom to be reinforced in a free and enjoyable way.

Sectioning off the playground

Often playgrounds consist of one open rectangular area. Apart from being visually austere, it does not have features that suggest different activities to children. Another problem is that the most active and aggressive behaviour can invade the space used by others – a main example as we have seen being the way children playing football can take up space, and knock into other children in the playground. Some children would prefer to sit and talk, others might prefer games with ropes or stones, others might like ring games, and so on.

One way of making the playground more attractive, as well as catering for such different activities, is to divide it up into separate areas.

A close examination of the playground area, perhaps drawn out to scale on paper, can suggest ways this might be done to good effect. For example, one part of the playground of one school was a narrow rectangular space between the school and a high external wall, and this served well as a fairly self-contained area for football. The footballers were happy because goal 'posts' could be made apparent, and the walls used, as in indoor five-a-side games, to pass the ball against. Another corner of the same playground housed a portable classroom, and there was a space between this and an external wall. Benches were purchased for this area in an attempt to create an area where children could sit down. There were plans to buy picnic tables as well. There was another area for skipping.

Staff in a middle school, as part of an attempt to cut down on squabbling and fights, had decided to 'carve out' the playground into different areas for games like football and netball, and to devote a small playground on the site to quieter activities like sitting, and strolling. Benches were supplied by the PTA.

The playground of another school had been divided into a number of areas. There was an adjoining field – a disused cemetery – that was used for football, there was a 'wild garden', there was a courtyard where children could talk and read if they wanted to escape the hurly-burley, and there was an asphalt covered area with a slide, a climbing frame and a fort.

Making the playground more attractive

It is a joy to enter a good infant or junior classroom. There can be an initial shock at the amount of colour and material to take in. Everywhere there is evidence on display of activities in progress or of writing or paintings completed. Here is a description of one, probably not untypical, classroom. On one wall there is a display on the story of Jack and the Beanstalk with children's written versions of the story, and paintings of characters, house and beanstalk. On other walls there are displays on the development of seeds to plants, letters of the alphabet, a display on the use of number lines as an aid to addition, and another on letters that can prefix 'at' in order to make words. In one corner there is a shop with a number of items with price tags that can be bought with 'pretend' money (though the totalling of the prices of items and change given involves real use of number operations). On one cabinet there is a display on capacity which involves plastic containers of different shapes and sizes, and on another cabinet, a display on different shapes and their names, and scales for weighing various objects. There is also a display of books, and work cards in boxes on maths and language work. From the ceiling hang children's paintings of plants, like colourful mobiles, with different parts labelled, and adults have to weave and duck to move around the classroom.

In the hall there are more displays. There are drawings of mini-beasts by reception and nursery children, a model made up of different shaped everyday objects, a display on 'living things', a display on 'things are happening in the pond', and another on stones and shells.

So much energy, collaboration and invention has gone into the look of the inside of the school. Yet by contrast playgrounds, even in schools with the most colourful interiors, are often dull and dingy, and defy every canon upon which good primary school practice has been founded.

As a very basic first step in improving the quality of life in the playground much more effort could be put into improving its look. There are a number of ways this is being done.

An inner city primary school, after discussions with children, and work on their 'ideal' playground, invited an artist to work with the children on a mural on an external wall of an area devoted to quiet activities. The theme for the mural came from the children; the advice about design and help with the application of paint came from the artist. There were also areas of the playground with plants cared for by the children. Staff were impressed at how, in a largely deprived inner city area, there had been no damage to the mural or the scaffolding in front. About the latter the head said ruefully: 'only one nudge would destroy it'.

In a similar vein, a nearby inner city school had put out 'planters'– sewage pipes cut, filled with earth and then planted with flowers. These were paid for out of school funds, though an application had been made to the LEA. Staff in this school were also impressed by the way children did not damage flowers.

Similarly, in another inner city infant school one long wall under a canopy had been designated for a mural, each section of which was to be completed by a different class and their parents.

Both staff and parents of one nursery school apparently felt that the exterior was rather grim because of the high brick wall that enclosed the tarmacadam-covered playground (Bhatia, 1987). Money was raised to commission an artist to paint a mural on part of the wall. This proved the inspiration for the creation of another mural, this time involving the children themselves in all stages of the project. They helped in the design stage, the choice and purchase of paint and equipment, and the scrubbing and white washing of the playground wall. Staff were impressed by their enthusiasm, energy and concentration. The children were apparently not daunted by the scale of the task. Subject matter ranged from a street lamp to a smug looking pig. The project seems to have been of great educational value to the children, as well as improving the playground environment (Bhatia, 1987).

Staff in a new junior school had become concerned about the outside area of their new school, largely as a result of thinking hard about the inside of the building when in consultation with the borough architect. Although compared to many inner city schools they had a lot of land, and there was a field and a stream on the site, they believed it could be improved. Children's views were canvassed. As a result they altered the area at the front of the school to make it more welcoming and useful for parents when they came to leave and collect their children. Thorn bushes that had shielded the school entrance were removed and the plan was to pave the area and provide seating for parents so that they were not forced to stand around and 'look embarrassed'.

This school – like many others – was plagued with a litter problem, and so staff had taken the step of banning crisps from the school premises, and installing large, camouflaged and lockable bins 'like those in National Parks'. This had reduced the amount of litter on the site.

Often the chance to make the playground more interesting is not seen. One head said that she had managed to stop, just in time, plans to asphalt over an area created by the demolition of outside toilets. She obtained permission to create a small garden. She wanted to go further and have low walls, sandpits, and wooden play equipment, but there was very little room, and there were also disagreements with the neighbouring junior school about how the playground could be best used.

One of the problems facing staff is that they are unclear what they might do and yet do not know where to turn for advice. Consequently, efforts to improve playgrounds are often piecemeal; for example, staff in nearby schools in the same authority could have similar discussions and problems and yet be unaware of each other and their efforts.

There are organizations which offer help to schools. Some schools in London have been helped by 'Interaction'– a charitable trust, founded by Ed Berman, the theatre director and community artist – which aims to set up self-help improvement projects with school children under the title of the 'Work to Play' project. Amongst the physical objectives of their work are the creation of a mural, concrete play structures, installing, painting and decorating planters, designing and marking out game lines on the ground, and painting in goal-posts and target games on walls. Participation of staff, children and parents, where possible, is a key feature of Interaction's approach; schools are told explicitly that they are buying more than the physical improvements. Self-help and 'constructive habits' are seen as important learning objectives and can help against vandalism.

Interaction describe their work as having four stages: first, discussions are held with staff, children and parents which will include descriptions of work in other schools and aims to arrive at agreement about the overall theme of work. A 'contract' is signed with children, stating that they will help with the work and maintenance. Secondly, the children select an aspect of the theme and work on models of the play structures and designs of the mural. Interaction staff then integrate these into a master model and drawing. Thirdly, the physical work is carried out, and fourthly, there is a planting ceremony and a plaque is 'unveiled'. This last stage aims to give a sense of pride to the children and make visitors aware of the project. Descriptions of Interaction's work in London schools can be found in Chappell (1986) and Baker (1987).

Another London-based project is the Islington Schools Environment Project. It began in 1977 with a collaboration between art teachers and staff and pupils in Laycock Primary School that attempted to bring art education out of colleges in order to involve school communities in transforming their playground environments. The main aim is to search for unique and creative solutions to barren playspaces and anonymous architecture. One of the team has written that one of the problems of 'collaboration' is to devise ways that really allow people to contribute to design solutions (Allan, 1986). This is a particular problem in the case of three-dimensional work, like play structures, with which children have little experience to draw on. The approach used at Penton Primary School was to work in a figurative way by designing a lizard out of car tyres. After a visit to the Hayward Gallery, and the loan of two live and one stuffed lizard, the children produced two-dimensional representations and a sculpture, which were then presented to the rest of the school at an assembly. A 20-foot long lizard, made of tyres, was then built at the ISEP workshops, and then installed in the playground. It was apparently a very popular plaything with the children. The ISEP has now produced a kit which aims to recreate the process of playstructure design, while producing workable structures.

Both these organizations, then, place a lot of importance on collaboration with staff, pupils and parents, not so much because it spreads the workload, but because of the positive attitudes and skills it can engender. Collaboration is something of a catch-all term, and difficult to work in practise, but it can provide the basis for fundamental changes not only to the appearance but also to attitudes toward the outside environment. There are other organizations that can offer advice to schools on physical improvements to the playground and some are referred to in appropriate sections below.

Apparatus in the playground and playground safety

If the problem with playgrounds is that children have nothing to do, then one answer is to provide apparatus for them to play with. In Chapter 3 we looked at the possible use of transportable equipment; here we are concerned with permanent equipment, fixed in the playground.

Imagine the reaction of a group of 11-year-olds who arrive at the playground in their local park and find within the fenced off area . . . nothing – no slide, swings, roundabouts or any other equipment at all. It is very doubtful that they would stay more than a few minutes. And it would not be surprising if they found other, possibly less acceptable, outlets for their energies. But imagine the situation still further: the children find 200 other children in the same situation. It may seem an unlikely scenario but this is exactly the situation in many school playgrounds.

Why are so many school playgrounds without play equipment? A major reason, again, is that we have simply got used to playgrounds as they are. Their lack of interest is a product of inertia. As one author has written: 'We are dreadfully conservative. A major advance is considered the dressing of conventional equipment in coloured stripes, or disguising a slide as a rocket' (quoted in Parnell and Ketterson, 1980). Another reason, commonly cited by staff in schools, is that they do not have the funds to buy equipment.

But there is a third reason, and this concerns safety in the playground, and worries in LEAs and schools about accidents to children in their care. We look first at the issue of safety, because it so closely affects playground design and equipment.

Concerns about safety have put a straightjacket over the ability of some schools to make playgrounds more interesting places. I visited one school which had what was clearly a dangerous climbing frame in its playground. It was not suitable for infants because its rungs were spaced too far apart and did not provide a secure enough hold for many children of this age group. It had been inspected by LEA officials, but had remained now for three years, unused. The children had been told often about the frame, and knew they were not allowed on it, but it must have been a source of considerable frustration – it being painfully obvious every playtime that they were not allowed near the one object in the playground that promised any fun!

Many playgrounds are barren areas of asphalt for similar reasons. The school staff and parents may have had ideas for improving the playground but have been advised by LEA officials that their plans are potentially hazardous.

And of course there must be real concerns about safety. The surfaces used for playgrounds are hard and children can receive bad knocks if they fall from apparatus. Research at Hospital Accident Departments indicated that 15 per cent of children treated in hospitals had sustained injuries in playgrounds, mostly at swings and climbing frames (reported in *The Leisure Manager*, 1986), though most of these accidents are likely not to be in school playgrounds. The issue of playground safety is understandably of concern to parents. Their awareness of the problems has been heightened by recent television programmes. A recent article in *Which?* (1988) reflected this concern and on the basis of an inspection of 139 playgrounds detailed some appalling safety hazards of playground equipment (though again, it is not clear how many of these were school playgrounds).

School staff have experienced the concern of parents. A delegation of parents went up to see the head in one school because they were worried about the potential dangers of children falling from equipment in the playground, and wanted the whole playground covered in a safety surface. The head estimated that this might cost as much as £100,000!

It is easy to sensationalize the problem, and to exaggerate the extent of the threat to children. The experience of another head was that most accidents were not in fact the result of falls from the climbing frame at all, but more likely the result of head to head clashes, caused by inevitable movement around the playground, and not looking where one was going. In a similar vein, the head of an inner city school found that the main problems were minor injuries, caused by seemingly inevitable accidental clashes around the playground. Another head thought that many injuries were caused by football games, and were not anyone's fault as such, but the result of vigorous movement and contact in a crowded space. These do not receive the same publicity in the media. They are also difficult to anticipate and guard against.

But staff, like parents, are of course worried about the hard ground under many climbing frames and other equipment in the playground. Siting equipment on grass is no answer; indeed, it may be dangerous because children may feel it is a soft surface, and take chances, when in fact it is only slightly less hard than tarmac, especially in winter. Children were barred from using a climbing frame on the grassed area of one first school for this reason. In my visits I found many staff interested in finding out more about the safety surfaces that have recently begun to appear on the market. There was interest in rubberized and wood chip surfaces in the hope that they might provide an answer to dangers of falls. (Advice on these matters can be found in Watson and Tipp, 1983, *Times Educational Supplement*, 8.1.88; Heseltine and Holborn, 1988.) All such plans encounter the same problem – the surfaces are very expensive. Some schools have managed to raise funds – or rather parents have done so – but others have simply put plans to one side. Heads could not usually get any help from their LEA (though see below).

In fact, school staff are in an invidious position when it comes to playground safety; they are blamed if anything goes wrong and yet they have very limited power and funds to make any changes in the playground. A tragic incident in a West London middle school highlights the problem. A child was knocked over in the playground and suffered a green stick fracture to her arm. The school staff responded immediately, summoning the parents to the school, and transporting the girl to hospital. Unfortunately, because of medical complications the child's arm became gangrenous and had to be amputated. But even this did not stop the infection and the girl died.

The staff in this school could not be blamed for the accident or the tragic consequences of it. But it highlighted for the head what a difficult position he was placed in. He was adamant, after his experience, that not enough attention is paid to playground safety. In particular, it is not something that can be left to schools to cope with on their own, or for parents to be left to raise money to provide expensive safety surfaces. The incident – though thankfully rare – indicated that it is more important than that. If there is to be an improvement in playgrounds, which would include more equipment (and all equipment has some potential danger attached to it), then there has to be a corresponding increase in attention and action on safety. And this has to extend beyond the individual school, and it has to involve the LEA, because their responsibility includes the plant and fabric of the school, and it involves funds and expertise that is beyond that which an individual school can provide. As the head said: 'They'd run a thousand miles in the opposite direction at the expense of it, but playground safety is not something that can be left to a school's ability to raise funds for safety surfaces.'

The issue of playground safety and the associated problems of funding therefore greatly affect the provision of equipment in playgrounds. They are important obstacles to any improvement in the playground environment, and explain the pessimism one often finds in many schools about the possibility of change. It can also depress parents' enthusiasm for fund-raising. Many feel themselves at an impasse.

This is a pity because there are now some exciting apparatus on the market, and thought has been given to apparatus that go beyond traditional climbing frames, slides and swings (e.g. see Phelps, 1984; Stadlen, 1974; *Times Educational Supplement*, 8.1.88; Heseltine and Holborn, 1988). Parnell and Ketterson (1980) offer a useful discussion of what playgrounds should offer, in the contect of a critique of playground designs in North America (see also Bowers, 1979).

I visited one junior school in Richmond which had an active group of parents who had initiated a phased programme to improve the playground. (The head said the playground was 'squalid'). They had researched equipment that was available and had chosen a climbing frame of wood with rope. Under the frame, rubberized safety tiles had been fitted. In other parts of the playground the parents had installed a very strong, and attractively coloured, wooden train, built in Germany. There was also an old oar-driven lifeboat, that had been used for television programmes, and was found to be a splendid prop for all sorts of games. There was a geometric climbing frame, play caves that were apparently very popular, and two miniature houses. Payment was provided by splitting costs three ways between parents, the LEA, and local charities. The parents' commitment had been sustained over a period of 12 years, which the head considered an achievement, especially considering that new parents had to be convinced as their children came into the school. The head was impressed with the generosity of parents (one parent had donated £200 for a bench).

Parents in this school found an impressive range of apparatus from which to choose. Another school has as a central focus of its playground a wooden model of the Polka Theatre in Wimbledon. This had not been purchased but built for the school, and to their designs, by a friendly carpenter. It was complete with a gallery, reached by a staircase, and an overhung upper storey, and was very popular. There was also in the playground a geometric frame, a slide, and concrete shapes. Access to the climbing equipment and the Theatre was not open to all at playtime, but only to the class of the teacher on duty. This arrangement kept numbers down to 25 or so children, and, as teachers' duties were on a rota basis, made sure everyone had a chance to go on the equipment.

The experience of staff in this school was that it is possible, with tenacity and a circle of useful parents and friends, to come up with exciting ideas for the playground. This was also seen in the playground of the school described above, where parents, with the advice of LEA staff, had built a large and dominating fort like structure made out of cut telephone cable poles.

It also worth bearing in mind that although bought-in equipment may be exciting, materials that offer most to children may be open-ended and manipulative. Research in the USA suggests that playground equipment should provide a wide range of experiences (see Parnell and Ketterson, 1980). Poole and Poole (1982) argue that although there is certainly a place for traditional playground equipment (like swings and slides) and that children still enjoy them, non-traditional play materials (for example, recycled items – they give the examples of a decommissioned fire engine, boats and automobile parts) can also meet basic learning needs.

It is possible to involve pupils in the design and positioning of playground equipment – indeed they are the exclusive consumers, as it were, and their voice should be heard. Some have sought to do this by projects such as asking children to device their own ideal playground. This can be a valuable and stimulating exercise, though as was said in Chapter 3, the limitation is that it can be rather remote from any real decisions about the playground. More effective will be schemes involving children in actual decisions to be made about specific parts of the playground or equipment.

Staff in a junior school as part of a TVEI Arts project, had worked in collaboration with a nearby secondary school on improvements to the playground. Part of the work involved research by the secondary pupils of playground 'culture'. The primary school children also worked with an Advisory teacher on the design of a large apparatus for the playground. The building of the structure would cost £2-3000, and still needed the approval of the LEA on safety grounds.

Worries about costs – as we have seen – are one reason why apparatus for the playground are not more widespread and more interesting. Another reason is that staff are lacking easily accessible advice about available equipment and safety surfaces. This also helps explain why improvements to the equipment in the playground involve isolated items of equipment; there is less thought given to the overall design and use of the playground as an educational resource. Part of the problem is that individual schools are largely left to identify their own problems and needs for the playground, and to then both design and finance any improvements. This contrasts with help and resources available for other parts of the child's school experience and the curriculum. Again there is a strong case for outside advice and assistance. I return to this point in Chapter 7.

But some LEAs do have schemes to help schools plan and finance improvements, and these give some idea of what can be achieved. Brent LEA has been eligible for Government Urban Programme Funding since 1983. The Programme is administered by the Department of the Environment, who provide a grant of 75 per cent to the total cost of each project approved. Schools in

Brent, that were within areas likely to receive Urban Programme funding, were invited by the LEA to submit proposals to utilize these funds, and submissions were considered by officers from the Education and Development Departments. Proposals had to show how pupils, parents and community would be involved, and how the project would enhance the school environment: first, projects which had been carefully designed and for which costings were available, secondly, projects which had been designed in some detail, and thirdly, projects which needed more design detail.

One of the four submissions which received the first category of funding is described here as an illustration of the kinds of schemes that can be devised after a careful collaborative effort by staff, parents, LEA staff and other groups with specialist knowledge. It includes playground equipment, but also other aspects of playground design discussed so far in this chapter.

The school concerned is The North West London Jewish School. The school suffered from common problems in the playground, for example with football and girls being effectively limited by the boys to less space, but in particular it was felt strongly that the playground was extremely dull. At that time it had only two obsolete climbing frames with no safety surfaces underneath. There was a separate nursery playground but the rest of the playground was undivided for children aged four to eleven years. Once a term the head, David Collins, and senior school staff met the executive of the parents' association in what was described by the head as a 'wide-ranging and convivial forum'. At one meeting, the parent vice-chair asked whether something could be done about the playground, and this set in train a project to improve the playground.

The school was fortunate enough to be adopted by an organization – Community Land and Workspace Services (CLAWS) – that gave them 35 hours of free planning time by one of their landscape architects. She spent her time at the school talking to children, staff, lunchtime supervisors, and parents. Her brief was to investigate the technical feasibility and cost of improvements to the school playground. As a result of discussions she identified the desire for play equipment for all ages, equipment for the nursery playground, designated areas for ball games including football and netball, quiet sitting areas, benches for sitting, and a wildlife garden, that would only be used when supervised. One reason for the garden was that the staff knew that a forthcoming HMI inspection report would recommend that more could be done on science education and it was thought that an environmental/wildlife area would be a field setting where scientific work could be conducted. Another more practical reason was to make better use of a 'buffer zone' that already existed between the school and neighbours, and which lay out of bounds and unused. Discussions were held with staff from the British Trust for Conservation Volunteers (BTCV) who offered advice, for example, on plants and suppliers' names, and supervision on the work itself.

The feasibility study took 18 months and produced sketches and drawings for schemes, technical information about play equipment and safety surfaces, and a list of suitable plants for the garden and playground. The estimated costs were in the region of £30-40,000! The head said 'when we picked ourselves up from the floor . . . we thought parents might be able to manage £5000 but they could not raise that kind of money. We did not know where to go next'.

The most expensive items in the estimate were £6000 for the supply and erection of play equipment, £3500 for the supply and erection of a timber play wall, £2500 for the supply and installation of a play train, £2172 for the supply and planting of shrubs and plants, £2000 for the supply and installation of nursery play equipment, and £3750 for the supply and laying of a rubber surface, including a tarmac base and edging to a depth of 29 mm.

It was at that point that the head received a letter from Brent LEA, informing him, along with other heads about a seminar on the environment project, and about the invitation to bid for the funds described above. Consequently, on the basis of the CLAWS estimate, a proposal was written and submitted to the LEA. The head said it was a fortuitous offer by the LEA, but that he did not think his application would be successful. He recognized that within the LEA there were many deprived communities and poor schools and that his own school had many middle class and professional parents, and so it was thought that the LEA would be unlikely to pass the submission. But to his surprise, he heard that they had been awarded a grant of £20,000 to begin work, which was made up of £15,000 from the DOE and £5000 from Brent LEA. The rest of the costs would have to be met by the parents. At the time of my visit the plans were out to tender.

It might be objected that the school is not typical, and, as we have seen, was relatively well endowed with funds. This is quite true, but there are still, I think, lessons that can be learnt from their experience. One of these is that friendly collaboration over an extended period between parents and school staff can greatly help in the drawing up of plans to improve the school. Another is that efforts should be made to seek advice from specialist groups. This need not be expensive. Both CLAWS and BTCV offered their services free. But perhaps the main lesson is the way that the LEA can provide a key role in the instigation of valuable work in school environs. At a time when LEAs in general, and Brent LEA in particular, are publicly criticized by the government and some sections of the press, this needs to be stressed.

Before we end this section it is worth sounding a note of caution. Choices about playground equipment in Britain do not often appear to be based on an informed view about likely use by children. This again contrasts with materials used in main curriculum areas. Playground equipment is a costly investment for a school, and yet decisions about outside equipment can be shots in the dark – the fairly low level hope being that children will like it. What is required is a sounder basis for choice of equipment in principles of child development and playground design. Brown and Burger (1984) have argued that much literature on playground environments in the USA makes recommendations not based on empirical support. Careful thought needs to be given to what changes will offer children, and what effects are expected in the quality of play. We must be on our guard. A single, large, expensive item of equipment may look good on paper, or in a brochure, but may, for example in the absence of proper organization of access to it, frustrate children, and play may break down.

It should not be assumed that all changes to the playground environment will automatically lead to more advanced and involved forms of play in children. A recent comparison in the USA of traditional and 'contemporary' playgrounds (that is, novel forms and shapes, pleasing arrangements, based on sand, concrete or wood) found that there was little difference in children's verbal interaction, social play, and cognitive play behaviour, and there was a tendency for less physical play (i.e. more sitting, standing and walking) in the 'contemporary' playground (Hart and Sheehan, 1986). The results are open to conflicting interpretations. The authors say that 'contemporary playgrounds may be less conducive . . . to active, developmentally advanced play behaviours . . .although the aesthetics of such playgrounds make them attractive to adults, the fixed structure of such ('contemporary') playgrounds may be masking an influence toward play passivity or inactivity' (p.669). This is a controversial view, and the results might just mean that 'contemporary' playgrounds settle children's behaviour in ways that many might view as a good thing. But this study does serve as a warning that a check must be kept on children's behaviour after any changes that have been made; even the most attractive looking designs and equipment may, from a child's point of view, offer few opportunities for play.

Another American study (Brown and Burger, 1984) also found that more comtemporary playground designs did not promote educationally desirable social, language or motor behaviours to any greater extent than more traditional playgrounds. It was concluded that designs were not fully developed in practice. The design aspects that did appear to be important were 'zoning' (positioning of equipment), 'encapsulation' (enclosing areas for separate activities), and the provision of appropriate materials (e.g. vehicles).

But a main claim of Brown and Burger's paper is that playground use is affected by the attitude of supervisors. The authors found that supervisors tended to interact with children only when a crisis occurred, and did not perceive the playground as an educational environment. They did not, therefore, get involved with, or enhance, playground behaviour.

Using the playground as a resource for learning

One detects a growing awareness of the potential of the outside area of a school as a resource in the development of an understanding about the environment. This was evident, for example, in the North West London Jewish School's submission, and in particular with regard to the contribution that could be made to the science curriculum by the wildlife/nature garden.

This is a way of looking at the playground that goes beyond its use as a setting for a short recreational period, and looks at it as an important educational setting, perhaps as a living exercise in conservation. To take up a worry expressed earlier about the contrast between the classrooms and the playground, there are signs that some are thinking imaginatively about the playground in ways that will extend the learning that can be stimulated in a primary classroom out into the playground. A useful report on changes and improvements that can make the playground a valuable curriculum resource, and its possible role in developing environmental awareness, is by Cherry Mares and Robert Stephenson (1987, now being revised).

Even modest efforts that might be all that can be afforded can be valuable. For example, tubs and planters, of the kind described above to make the playground more atractive, can be a valuable resource, especially in cities, where contact with the natural world of plants and animals can be limited.

A middle school, as part of a PTA initiative had a garden area with trees, rockery and flowers. This was tended by the Parks Department but each class was responsible for a couple of tubs each. The head was keen to extend this, because it was felt children benefited from the commitment.

As you enter the grounds of one West London infant school a sign says: 'You are entering a conservation area'. The head explained how it had started. The school had an association with the grounds of Chiswick House, using their open green area. On the staff of the maintenance staff was a man who was keen to encourage schools as ecological areas. The head contacted Norwood Green – a local centre for ecological studies – and with their help drew up plans for the school grounds. With the help of one of maintenance staff and students, ponds were dug out. Parents had raised money for the pond lining, and also a hedge. They helped plant bushes, and bulbs. During the gales in October 1987 a willow tree had blown down; logs from this were now used to encourage insects and fungi. Also, during an initiative to plant trees, the children had clubbed together in order to buy a replacement tree, and had had a photograph of the planting of it in the local paper. The head said it was definitely not a play area, but rather a place to encourage an understanding of their natural environment.

Clearly many, especially older, schools have inherited outside areas that cannot easily be made conducive to conservation/wild life. Many are completely covered in ashphalt, for example. Much can be done, however, in making good use of school grounds at the design stage of new shools. One school had recently been moved to a new site. It was a handsome building in a generously proportioned plot, with many established shrubs and trees. There was a field, a pond area with reeds (where children went under supervision), a hard-covered area where a climbing frame would go, a shrubbery with a sturdy rhododendron which children used to swing and climb on, a 'wild' area, and hens and cockerels.

It must be said, though, that designs for new schools do not always make good use of the outside area. Staff and pupils in one junior school had recently moved from a small Victorian school to a new purpose-built site. While the head was generally happy with the building itself, and some of their ideas had been taken on board, the playground had not been so well planned. In contrast to the previous school, it was a hill-top site, exposed to the wind in winter and to the sun in summer. There were no sheltered shaded areas, and again in contrast to well-established games in the old school, there were no walls to bounce balls off. Paths were not wide enough, and in consequence grass had been trampled away to leave ugly borders of bare earth. An area designed as a quiet area, was at the lowest point in the playground, and often too wet to use. An elaborate semi-circular set of stairs, that was designed to also provide seating from which to view outside performances was never used for this purpose because it was too exposed and in any case the weather could not be trusted. The head said that when the children first moved in they dashed around the new open space in an uncontrolled way. Later, a small section of brick wall was built in the middle of the playground, to throw balls against, but it was a forlorn sight and in general the head felt a valuable opportunity had been missed.

There are many developments initiated by schools, or by local authorities, not mentioned here, that make good use of the school grounds as an educational resource. Their experience would suggest that anyone contemplating improvements should find out if there are local organizations which can offer help, for example, the area Wildlife Trust. The Urban Spaces Scheme (Polytechnic of North London, Holloway Road, London, N7 8DB) publishes a number of useful pamphlets, for example on creating school nature gardens. Some other publications and useful organizations are given by Mares and Stephenson (1987).

Just one cautionary note. The creation of conservation areas in the playground may not always be to the advantage of children. In most schools I visited, conservation areas were only visited under supervision and at certain times during the school day. This is understandable, given the fragility of plants, insects and so on there. But one can imagine the frustration of children at playtime if this means making a (possibly already small) playground even smaller, with a previously accessible area now out of bounds!

Many initiatives in schools are fragmented and of variable quality. The Learning Through Landscapes Project has been doing important work in pooling experience nationwide and establishing criteria of good practice in the design, management and use of school grounds. Jointly funded by the Department of Education and Science, the Countryside Commission, and Berkshire, Hampshire and Surrey County Councils, it set out to investigate the potential of school grounds as a resource for learning and teaching, investigate design and management practices relating to school grounds, and report on the design, management and use of school grounds in relation to improving environmental quality and educational opportunity. A part of the project is the recording of initiatives in schools, and the extrapolation of key ideas which can be of use in schools generally. A report on this is expected in 1989.

But there are probably few initiatives as interesting or challenging as that at the Coombes infant school, in the village of Arborfield in Berkshire. This encapsulates many of the most exciting attempts to improve the playground environment, and it is fitting to end this chapter with a more detailed look at it.

The head has written, to accompany a video made about her school:

> It is sad to reflect that the most impoverished of immediate personal landscapes, from the child's point of view, is that of the school environs. We have in the main been willing to accept a bleak uniformity – easily mown grass, tarmac, and the occasional rose bed – as the setting for education and other public institutions. We should rather be offering the children aesthetic delight in their school grounds, places of colour, richness and diversity which may be used for recreational purposes, imaginative play and for learning. The scope for environmental education 'on the doorstep' is enormous.

A visit to the Coombes school shows just how much can be made of the school environment. It shares the site with a junior school. Both schools lie on the side of a road on the outskirts of the village.

Behind are fields, woodland and, further still, the army barracks where many of the children at the school live.

It is not a particularly large site, and the school buildings are not very striking. But the environs of the infant school certainly are. One gets a sense of its uniqueness on first sight; an impression that was not dispelled when for the first time in my experience the head – Sue Humphries – asked the caretaker to show me around. One soon saw why. The caretaker had played a major part, along with other members of the school 'family', in the formation of the garden.

It is hard to believe that 16 years ago this was a bare plot with just the school buildings. Now it is a marvellous place, dense with trees, plants, animals, and play equipment. Every November, trees are planted by the children. They include maple, silver birch, lime, Lombardy poplar, and apple trees. They have concentrated on fruit trees because the produce can be used by the children. There are also Christmas trees and Norway spruce that are ceremoniously felled. Trees are coppiced to provide ground cover and break up sight lines.

Spring bulbs are planted by the children in the autumn. Every child plants at least two snowdrops, two crocuses, two aconites, and two daffodils. These flowers do not offer much to conservation but the planting, picking and giving of flowers can help show what the immediate natural world can provide, as well as give pleasure to the picker and to those to whom they are given. One of the most important parts of the garden are the compost heaps. Those at the Coombes are taken very seriously because it is recognized that they provide the garden with its strength and life. They are large ones, comprised of leaves brought in by the refuse collection service, one suspects with a little gentle persuasion by Sue Humphries. Samples are inspected by the children in order to identify worms and insects that help to rot it down. Children can examine at close hand change and decay, and they can see the process of recycling at work.

There are three aquatic habitats – two formal ponds and a shallow clay-lined basin which will gradually revert to marsh area.

There is a smallholding with bantams and sheep. There were cockerels roosting in the trees. The caretaker and his family played a key role in feeding the animals and looking after them at weekends and during the school holidays. There was also an owl box, and owl chicks have been hatched and reared there. Bird and bat boxes have been situated by the children throughout the school grounds.

Peas and beans are planted in patches of cleared ground and are tended in the medieval way, that is to say, weeds and crops are allowed to flourish together. They do surprisingly well. A feature of the gardens is the sunflowers. Four months after sowing they have outgrown everything. The children are encouraged to see, touch and examine the shells, and the sunflowers are ritually collected on 'sunflower harvest day'. Jerusalem artichokes – a form of sunflower, but with edible roots – are also grown. The children are encouraged to sample the roots, usually in their raw state, and in the same way the children take part in the picking of rhubarb and potatoes, and learn about how the leaves are toxic, while the stems and roots are edible. Rhubarb is used in jams and chutney, or cooked with sugar. Potatoes are also cooked and eaten. Green tomatoes are used in chutney. The children learn about the way that changing the state of fruit can aid storing. Pumpkins are grown in humus-rich soil, and are gathered in the traditional way. Children are interested in the skin, flesh and seeds, and, it seems, rather surprisingly like the bland taste of the flesh.

The garden houses a range of other habitats. There is a bog garden, created by exploiting the natural clay, and then covering this with moss peat to retain water. Plants were then planted by teachers and children. At the time of my visit a deep ditch had been dug. And heat and humidity traps were provided by the laying down of old, biodegradable carpets throughout the grounds.

These are the sights one sees during a visit to the school. It is interesting and pleasing to the eye, but it is much more than that. In order to appreciate the garden one has to understand the view about the education of young children which has guided its creation. This attempts to show children how all living things have their bases in the soil, and ultimately return there. It shows children the development and cycle of life spans, and methods of regeneration. Key points in the year – such as planting and harvesting – are celebrated, almost ritually, to show their real and symbolic place in this process.

There is a dual focus. An understanding of the natural world is seen as important and enjoyable in its own right, but it is also the basis for the acquisition of linguistic, scientific and mathematical skills. As Sue Humphries has said:

> The natural rhythms of life – as we experience them in our immediate landscape – can and do touch us if we make provision for them to do so. We are endeavouring to provide an environment which will stimulate, satisfy and enhance the whole person – which will give scope to the emergent scientist, the latent mathematician and the budding linguist. In short, to give scope to that part of everyone which is sensitive, discerning and appreciative.

The aim is to involve children directly. For example, they learn about the life-cycle of the common frog by direct observation of tadpoles in the pond. They then might view diagrams illustrating the life-cycle, and have the task of helping to construct a diagram which economically organizes – in words – the information they have learned. Prior to this the children would have looked at books in their classroom on amphibian life-cycles. Thus the aim is for children to come upon scientific generalizations in the context of their own experience. The recording of information is preceded by direct observation and directed discussion.

There is a heavy emphasis on direct sensory experience – through seeing and touching plants and animals. For example, the children lifted the biodegradable carpets and, to great excitement, found there three families of bank voles. On occasions the children are encouraged to pick up and touch the voles, but routinely, examination is done by eye only. The belief is that it is in this way that children will develop a respect for, and an interest in, the natural world.

Play is far from neglected. Indeed some visitors are most impressed by the provision for it outside the school. There are tyres bolted together and two boats for imaginative play. There is a tunnel with a surprise entrance, tree trunks and a traveller's caravan that has been the subject of interest, and about which its previous owner, a traveller, calls each year, to talk to the children and show them how to groom his horse. There are game markings on hard covered areas for play, and a separate area in a corner for skipping, with illustrated rhymes painted on the wall.

The staff take the 'stewardship of public property', as they call it, very seriously. Their view is that by improving and developing this land, the whole community will benefit, for example, by creating a visual amenity (a site where trees and bushes are arranged so as to resemble areas of old countryside), and providing a sanctuary for some of those creatures and plants that are not welcome in a small private garden or town park (forest trees, nettles, thistles, moles, etc.).

The work at Coombes County Infant school illustrates what can be done with the school environs. The head is not surprised that schools have problems with children's behaviour in the playground if those playgrounds are barren and impoverished. One can hardly expect respect for an environment that offers children nothing.

The staff at Coombes have broken down the barriers between classroom and outdoors, in order to combine both in an all embracing cross-curricular philosophy. It would be a mistake to think that all this has been easy, and only possible in a safe, predominantly middle-class village. In fact, the children in the school are mostly from the army garrison, and there is a lot of disruption caused by movement of families, and anxiety caused by service, particularly in Northern Ireland. The garden has come about through two things: first, the shared inspiration and clear vision of Sue Humphries and her staff about the education of young children, and secondly a good deal of hard work, especially by the caretaker. Not everyone would accept the head's views in their entirety, and not many, I suspect, would feel able to devote so much of their (and their caretaker's!) energies in this way. Some may also feel that children can learn the concepts encouraged at Coombes during the course of more traditional classroom based activities. But it challenges us, I believe, to think carefully about the school grounds, and can offer ideas about how schools can be improved. On a continuum of efforts to make the playground an educational resource, it is the top end of a scale on which others might judge their own efforts.

6
Alternatives to Fixed Period Playtimes

Given the problems with playtime that have been described in this book it is pertinent to consider whether there are any viable alternatives to the traditional arrangement of children having to go out, weather permitting, for a short recreational break in the morning and afternoon and a longer one at lunchtime. In this chapter we consider such alternatives.

Giving children choice about going out

We have seen in Chapters 1 and 2 that for some children playtime can present problems. One humane arrangement would be to allow children choice about whether or not to go out to the playground. Children could then stay in their classrooms if they wished, getting on with their work, reading, drawing and so on. This may seem like an obvious solution but in most schools there seems to be no choice about going out into the playground. One reason for this is because allowing choice means that the inside of the school, as well as the playground, has to be supervised, and so more staff would have to be on duty. Another worry is whether cover would be adequate within schools, should there be an accident and a claim by parents.

Some schools allow a partial choice about going out. In a south London infant school, for example, one classroom stayed open every day at lunchtime, and a supervisor (described by the head as 'marvellous') was on duty to provide activities like construction toys, sticking, sewing, and dressing up. In summer they might go outside and take books to read, or hear a story. It was designed to cater for those children who did 'not want to rush around', and as many as 35 to 40 children could be involved.

In a middle school, lunch ended at 1.15 but children were allowed to come into school if they wanted at 12.45. There was not a formal arrangement for supervision of children who decided to come in to school, but teachers could well be around at that time, for example, going to their classrooms to prepare for the afternoon, and the head and deputy head patrolled the school at intervals. The system was open to abuse, because of the thinness of supervision, but staff did not feel there were too many problems.

A first school allowed a 'free flow' of children to go to the medical room at lunchtime, on the most 'trivial of excuses'. It was seen as a way of allowing children to come into the school if they were finding life in the playground too difficult. 'They have a cuddle, and then go out again.'

In another school, top junior children were allowed a lot of flexibility. 'They have a privilege. Many don't go out – they read in the library, do writing, make bookmarks. Some are constructing a comic and duplicating it. We allow them initiative, and there is no trouble.'

The impression gained in the last school was that the top juniors at least welcomed the choice over whether or not to go out to the playground. In an unpublished survey of the views of 591 children, conducted by a group of heads in Leicestershire, it was found that a considerable proportion would have preferred to stay in at the dinner break – over 50 per cent of the girls and 36 per cent of the boys. Allowing choice does seem a fair and considerate way of organizing playtime. No matter how attractive a playground, and no matter how good the supervision, there are undoubtedly going to be children who would prefer to stay in their classrooms or in the library. Indeed, given the small proportion of the school day that is spent in reading activities (only two per cent in London infant schools, see Tizard *et al*, 1988) this might be one way of boosting the amount of time spent in reading. But – as the Leicester heads reluctantly concluded – given the present staffing ratio at lunchtime such a choice is not possible.

I have been able to find only a few schools that have allowed choice on a more complete basis, that is, for all the school and for all breaks.

Most heads I have spoken to have said that for practical reasons they could not allow choice. Some heads were horrified at the prospect, one saying that her boys would take advantage of it and cause havoc in the school. Another worry was that if allowed into another classroom children might easily upset and spoil the work going on there. But some of the concerns about supervision are not insurmountable. For example, during morning and afternoon play it would be possible for supervision to be doubled, so that one teacher could be on duty outside in the playground, and one inside. And supervision in school might be made easier by constraining children to one or two rooms. Staff would have to accept the extra supervision, but it would, after all, still mean that the majority could have a break.

It certainly seemed to work well in one infant school, where the head spoke warmly about the arrangement of giving children choice that she had introduced after coming from a school in another authority which had an integrated day and no playtime. All the schools in her present LEA, East Sussex, by contrast, had playtimes. She found that many upsets were caused by playtime and so the children could come in and get on with class work, read, play musical instruments, or whatever – no special break activities were provided. It was found that the top infants tended to get on with work, while the younger children continued playing. The head said: 'They were boisterous at first, but it calms down quickly – within one week. It helps so much – when the children know they haven't got to go out. There are no accidents, touch wood! There is far less unhappiness.' The numbers of children who went out varied from day to day, usually because of the weather. If it was sunny very many went out. Some children never went out, and conversely some never stayed in. Supervision was provided by one teacher outside, and one inside, the school.

No fixed period playtimes

Allowing children choice about whether or not to go out to play still leaves intact the timetabling of playtimes. A more radical departure is not to have fixed period playtimes at all, but to allow class teachers and their children to decide if and when they would like to use the playground.

Let us see how this works in one school in South London. Here the children do not as a rule go out to playtime, either in the morning and afternoon or at lunchtime. The children tend to stop work mid-morning and gather together for a chat, singing and milk, so there is a break from the routine of the classroom. The present head of the school had inherited the system from the previous head – Wendla Kernig, now a Lecturer at the Institute of Education, University of London. When Wendla arrived at the school she felt there was a lot of bad behaviour and she felt that fundamental changes needed to be made. She decided to scrap fixed period playtimes altogether. She said to me that she had hated playtime when she was a girl at school, and that she could see no reason for playtime at all.

It was not an isolated decision. It was part of a general view about education which tries to go beyond demarcations between different subjects, and between 'lessons' and recreational breaks. For Wendla and her staff, the starting point was a clear view about how children best learn. They felt that children work best not from an imposed, but from a negotiated curriculum, within which they pursue their individual work at their own pace and in terms of their own ability. With increased motivation, children need to work for extended periods on their work, without interruptions. Wendla said:

> You must clear from your mind the idea of a break. Think in terms of having a chunk of time – say 9 to 3.30. Forget about the breaks. There are some things one can't negotiate, for example going to the loo, having a drink, sitting down for a cigarette. But there's no need to go out at the same time, and it doesn't matter when you have it. And it doesn't have to be for 15 to 20 minutes. You must ask what are we trying to achieve? How do children learn? How does a young child learn to walk or to talk? They don't need a break!

It was the head's clear impression that behaviour in school had improved. She felt there were no behaviour problems – 'absolutely none' – and there were no problems outside. There was nothing to stop children and staff using the playground, but they rarely did so. She admitted that it was redundant. The children preferred to stay in. She described the children as more relaxed, there was a quiet hum of activity, and the stress on staff had decreased. Wendla was horrified when she saw what went on in playgrounds of schools she visited. She could see no justification for it.

How did it work in practice? Children aged five to eight years were vertically grouped, as were children aged eight to 11 years. Children were in groups of 50 to 60 with two teachers, a full-time helper and a parent helper. The head insisted that one teacher in each team be male and one female because she felt that it was important for young children to be taught by both sexes. The children went to lunch with their teachers – which took 20 minutes or so – and then returned to the classroom, perhaps for a story or to get on with their own work.

The arrangement was based, therefore, on the educational grounds that children should not be interrupted in an arbitrary manner from their work, making it difficult for them to pick up the same degree of involvement after the distractions of playtime. The arrangement should mean that schools do not suffer the abrupt change that often occurs between classroom activity and playtime, and there were none of the problems of preparing children for the playground that takes up so much time, especially with young children who need assistance with coats, buttons and toggles. Moreover, the system has the virtue, appealing no doubt to many, that there is no such thing as 'wet play' and all the problems of supervision that accompany it.

Most staff have an immediate and understandable worry about this arrangement – how can they get a break from continuous teaching? In the school just described, ancillary staff brought coffee to teachers where they happened to be teaching. With a team-teaching arrangement, with helpers paired with teachers, it was possible for staff to get away when they wanted for five to ten minutes to make a phone call, go to the loo, or see the head.

But there is another worry – surely the children will get edgy being indoors all day and don't they therefore need to dash around for a while in the playground? Wendla Kernig said that was left to teachers, so that there was nothing to stop the class going into the playground if they wanted. However, as has been said, children rarely wanted to go out. Wendla Kernig is not convinced by the 'letting off steam' function of playtime. To her, if children need to let off steam it suggests that all is not well with what is happening within school. If the work is varied and involving enough there is simply no need for an imposed recreational break; it is an anachronism.

There is a third worry. If children do not go out into the playground will this not mean that traditional games and rhymes will not be passed on from child to child? Wendla's answer to this worry is two-fold: first, if there are worries about playtime behaviour then clearly all is not well anyway with children's play, and secondly there are opportunities for games and rhymes within school and before and after school (the school operated an extended day with a play centre after 3 p.m.).

So much for the way the system worked in one school, and the reactions of the head to some common worries. Some other heads were sympathetic to the idea. For example, a head of an infant school contrasted the approach with the way the outside area is used in nursery schools and classes. There children can use the resources of the outside area as an extension of the classroom; and there is not a clear distinction drawn between them in the way one finds even in infant schools. The good nursery school therefore provides a model of the way infant and junior playgrounds can be used.

Another head felt that playtime interrupted activities in the class and many children did not like playtime and would not go out unless they had to. She felt it was more for the teachers benefit than the children. They needed to go to the loo and have a drink – indeed the head felt it was important that teachers did have a break from their classrooms. She had not been tempted to change present arrangements for that reason.

But the arrangement with no fixed playtimes is not commonly found. Why? To some extent the answer is that it deviates fundamentally from a tradition which by and large we have all come to accept as the norm, and so staff are reluctant to change it. But there are more precise worries, and perhaps most qualified to describe them are those in schools where an arrangement with no fixed playtimes has been tried.

The experience of one first school head is instructive. Prior to taking up this post she had been 11 years in a school in another LEA that did not have a fixed morning and afternoon break, though it did have a normal lunchbreak. It was an open plan school, divided into three 'suites', each consisting of three teachers and 90 children. The reasons for scrapping playtime were on similar educational grounds to those put forward by Wendla Kernig, that is, it interfered with the flow of children's work and ideas. There were also some children from a social priority housing estate, and the head of the school apparently put it to his staff that they would have difficulties controlling some of these children in the playground. The teachers had a break from continuous teaching by one of the three covering for the other two, and supervising the children for milk for 15 minutes. That teacher was then freed for a further ten minutes when the other two returned.

The head said the system did have its difficulties but 'we came to believe in it'. But then, after 11 years, the school had a new head who was not at all sympathetic to the system and immediately reverted to traditional fixed breaktimes, signalled by bells. So the head had the valuable opportunity of working with both systems that were, in a sense, imposed by different heads. She said she was surprised. It was only once she had been freed from the system that she realized fully the timetabling difficulties with it. Covering for others did interfere with work. In retrospect she was not sure that the children did pursue their work with more involvement, and manage resources more independently, in line with the original reasoning. Furthermore, with the traditional break there is a 15 minute absence from work in the classroom; in their system there was in effect a 25 minute break (that is, 15 + 10 minutes), when no work was being done. With a stable staff and no absentees the system could work well; with rapid turnover of staff, as there was in the school at the time, it became very fraught. Supply teachers were understandably unsure. The practical difficulties of the system bogged it down. It was simply more efficient for children and teacher to have a 15 minute break together.

The reaction of the children was interesting. On the whole they were reported to prefer going out to play. True, for the first time there were knocks and bumps, but they did not want to go back to the old system. They liked meeting friends, especially from other classes, and not having to find work to do in the class. They liked the freedom of movement, and also just the license to be idle, if they wanted. Interestingly, in view of Wendla Kernig's comments, the children seemed not to have been satisfied with the opportunities for really letting off steam. They saw a difference between the teacher controlled opportunity that had previously existed and the greater freedom allowed by the traditional playtime. Particularly troubling, in view of the original philosophy behind the plan, was the impression that in fact *more* work was achieved with fixed period playtimes. The children seemed to like having a deadline by which they had to finish work. It could be used to spur children on, and the threat of missing playtime used as a sanction.

The reaction of teachers was apparently also favourable. They did not like the new responsibility of playground duty, but they did find rewarding contact with more children in the school than were in their particular 'suite'. They also saw another side of their own children to that seen in the classroom. All in all the head said she would not like to work the system again, and had not introduced it into her current school.

In my search for schools which had a system of no fixed playtimes I contacted several only to find that they had reverted to a traditional playtime. For example, I was told about one school, but found they had changed back when the new head arrived a year ago. Interestingly the new head had been excited by the system; it was the staff who wanted to change back. In order to relieve teachers, one member of a two-teacher team had taken the whole group of about 54 children, and it was felt children were spending too much time in large groups. Staff also missed the camaraderie of the staffroom. But the new head was clearly not happy with the traditional playtime, and now that there were more adults in the school thought they might be able to try the system again.

I also visited two schools in one East London borough where they had reverted to traditional playtimes. In the first, the present head took up post seven years ago and the school did not have a mid-morning playtime. The head liked the arrangement because there was not an 'exodus' to the playground, there was continuity and involvement in work, and she felt the children were happy, and moved around enough in the course of their activities, and PE in school. 'It was a wonderful idea educationally.' While teachers had a break, two patrolled the school, along with ancillary staff, and supervised the classrooms.

However, two years ago they 'regretfully changed to fixed period playtimes'. This was principally because of several incidents at playtime. Some parents asked troubling questions about who was in charge during the times when children were in school, and not all classrooms could be supervised. The head felt the system was a good one, and would be possible with ancillary help in each class.

In the other school, the present head took up post two-and-a-half years ago to also find that there was no break in the morning or afternoon. For the first hour there was 'choice time' which included play with bricks and other equipment, and activities in the playground if wanted. There was not seen to be a need for playtime because children had been active long enough and could now sit down for more sedentary, academic work. But the new head did not like the rigidity of 'choice time', for example, because of the way activities like hearing children read did not occur then. She preferred an integrated approach, in the sense of not having fixed periods for 'choice' and then work. So, because the early morning activities could now be sedentary, playtime had been reintroduced. In any case, the head felt that playtime was important for children. If they did not get out then tempers could get frayed.

One teacher in the school put it like this: 'there's 35 in the class – imagine adults in a room with 35 others all day – they'd want a break'.

Clearly nothing conclusive can be deduced from these accounts. No system is ever without its problems, and the 'success' of it may well depend on the original attitudes of the teaching staff themselves, as much as the arrangement. The apparent success of the system of Wendla Kernig's school had much to do with the commitment, mutual agreement and support amongst staff, and perhaps, most importantly, the clear and strong views of the headteacher. From their point of view about how children best learn, playtimes simply had no place. It was a logical step to scrap them, and the children seem to have worked and behaved well as a result. However, others do not share the same philosophy about education and so the scrapping of playtimes may not work as well. One suspects that the perceptions of the two East London heads of what seemed to be very much the same arrangement was affected by their own views on appropriate approaches to learning and distinctions between work and non-work. The first head found playtimes fraught and difficult to supervise but was forced against her better judgement to reintroduce them; the second head changed to playtime because at heart she felt it valuable for children.

Much depends on the attitude of staff to the importance of having a fixed period break away from their children. I met some teachers who were not bothered by this, being quite happy to be with their class for the whole morning and afternoon (though they might well want a lunchbreak). Others felt they benefited from having a break mid-morning and mid-afternoon from the children. If staff are to be relieved so that they can get away for a few minutes then much will depend on the arrangements to relieve them. Some, like the first East London school, clearly had problems of supervision. Wendla Kernig's experience suggests that these practical problems are not insurmountable; for example, it is possible to so arrange things so that staff can get away if they wish. Nevertheless, it does seem that team teaching in open plan schools, preferably with full-time ancillary help, lends itself more easily to relieving teachers, because it is relatively easy for others to take over care of their children.

In view of the different views about alternatives to fixed period playtime, there is a need for more systematic evaluation of different ways of organizing the school day. We take this point up in Chapter 7.

Cutting out afternoon playtime

If there is one break which staff find most disruptive to activities in the school, it is that in the afternoon. The afternoon session is usually shorter by an hour or so than the morning session and there is thus less time in class, either side of the break. It can mean that there is little more than half an hour after returning from playtime before the end of the school day, and this severely constrains the range of activities that can be done. There may only be time for a story.

Some schools have therefore decided to reorganize the afternoon session so that there is no playtime. One head said: 'it was too short – a waste of time. The children would get fully involved and then would have to stop'.

Another head was quite clear that: 'children work better in the afternoon if they work right through. There is more effective learning. It's better if they don't go out – so we cancelled afternoon play, and we made lunchtime play longer (in order to finish the school day at the same time)'. Another head said that the afternoon playtime had been scrapped on the educational grounds that it interrupted the children's activity. But one unforeseen problem was that the adjoining junior school still had afternoon play, and 'they now interrupt us!'

But not everyone feels this way about afternoon play. Some took the general view that playtime was a valuable experience for children, and this included afternoon play. There are more specific reasons. When the head of one middle school took up his post the school did not have an afternoon break. But he felt the children in this school were not able to sustain their attention for an unbroken two hour stretch, and so reintroduced it.

This indicates that it is difficult to generalize about the advantages and disadvantages of cutting out afternoon play, because much will depend on the children in the school, and the perceptions staff have of their needs and ways of maintaining concentration.

Shortening the lunchbreak

Cutting out the afternoon playtime is part of a process of attempting to overcome problems that arise by cutting down on the time spent in the playground. Given that most problems seem to occur at lunchtime (see Chapter 4), it would be a logical extension to cut down on the amount of time spent in the lunchbreak.

Many of the schools I visited were doing, or had done this. There was a strong feeling, probably common in many schools, that a lunch break of 1¼ to 1½ hours is simply too long. It could well be profitably shortened by 15 to 30 minutes.

The head and deputy head of one junior school told me that ten years ago lunchtime was 'absolute hell'. With 480 children outside, and a lunchbreak that started at 12.00 and finished at 1.25, there were children who were scared of going outside. An educational psychologist was brought in to help identify and measure sources of conflicts. The first move was to knock off ten minutes. But there was still 'mayhem'. 'The sheer level of noise with beyond 300 children gets out of control.' There were many problems in the last 15 minutes in particular, with 'fights and conflicts, and dinner ladies unable to cope.' So the head approached the governors and it was agreed to shorten playtime by another 20 minutes, making it now only 55 minutes in length.

There are a number of practical problems that arise when a decision is taken to shorten playtimes. If the hours spent in the classroom remain unchanged then the school day will end earlier. There can then be problems for parents who may have jobs or commitments that make it difficult for them to get to the school earlier in the afternoon. They may also have more than one child at different schools, and it can be inconvenient if they end at very different times. However, these need not be a problem for all parents. It was the experience of the head of the school just mentioned, that the majority of parents and children preferred shorter lunchtimes and an earlier finish. And it is possible for schools to agree on finishing times.

There are practical limits on how much the lunchbreak can be reduced, assuming that children will be eating a dinner. In some schools with a lot of children, or with a small dining room, there may be two sittings, and it can be difficult to get through both in much less than an hour. Young children are often assumed to want to eat their food at great speed, but as many parents know, some can be very slow eaters. Even schools that organize lunch on a 'rolling' basis, with children or classes coming into the dining hall as others finish, can still have children in the dining hall for a large proportion of an hour. In one school the lunchbreak was reduced to 45 minutes, and the head did not think it could be reduced any further.

The 'continental day'

A logical extension on the policy of cutting back on lunchbreak, and one way of getting around problems about supplying children with lunch is to do away with the lunchbreak altogether. In essence this is what is usually meant by the so-called 'continental day'; that is, the school day would probably begin before the present starting time to start at around 8 a.m. and finish around 1.00 p.m. One head reflected that there was little about lunchtime to commend it and speculated about the possibility of an alternative arrangement of the school day. At present the morning session was from 9 to 12 and the afternoon session from 1.00 to 3.30 p.m. This amounted to 5½ hours in school. A start time of 8 would mean they could finish at

1.30 p.m. There could be two 15-minute breaks, and no lunch-break. But in practice the head could not envisage a change to a school day like this, mainly because of the outcry from parents.

There are several reasons why this way of organizing the school day is coming more and more into consideration as a possible option. One reason is the decline in the numbers of children who have school dinners. A survey conducted for the Labour Party in 1988 showed that between 1979 and 1987 the number of primary school children taking school meals had dropped by 41 per cent, while school rolls had only fallen by 14 per cent.

In addition, the introduction of Family Credit in 1988 has removed the entitlement of poor children to free school meals. It is widely expected that this will further reduce the numbers of children who will have school meals.

It must be said that there would be immense problems in a shift toward the continental day, but, before we look at them, let us first see what advantages the system could have. One way to do this is to look at the experience of a school that has adopted it. One school which pioneered the 'continental day' was recently commended by HM inspectors (reported in *Times Educational Supplement*, 25.3.88). It was concluded that its use in Tideway School in East Sussex 'works efficiently and is well-liked by pupils and teacher'. It was one of the first to operate classes from 8.10 a.m. to 2.15 p.m. with a 20-minute break at the end of the fourth period and a 35-minute break for lunch after the sixth period. It has been running for seven years. Reported advantages include the establishment of a better learning environment, particularly in later lessons in the day, and fewer behavioural problems out of class. Pupils particularly liked the idea of being able to arrive home early and complete homework before tea. Little adverse parental reaction was reported after the pilot year.

This is a secondary school which sets homework. There must be more cause for concern about children in primary schools returning home early to possibly empty houses, and without something to occupy them. It will also be noticed that the arrangement at Tideway School actually included a short break for lunch. In fact, what this school has is a school day that starts earlier than normal, but is otherwise similar to most schools with two playtimes. In practice, there does not appear to be a clear distinction between the 'continental day' and the traditional school day.

Several heads had considerable sympathy with the idea of not having a lunchbreak at school. One said: 'Frankly I would like to have 8 to 1.' It was her view that after the end of the morning at school 'other' staff could take over, and children could do activities related to their 'hobbies'. It was also her view that 'school meals have nothing to do with education'. What is being claimed here is that it would be a better use of the school building to have the school day concentrated in the morning, and then have other non-teaching staff take over, to provide lunch and then other hobby and craft activities in the afternoon.

Another head, who had earlier commented on the many problems that could arise at lunchtime, had begun to question whether a formal lunchbreak with a set time for eating was relevant anymore. She said that families do not tend to sit down together for a meal in the way they once did, and she was not sure it needed to be provided at school.

It is important to make the point that the term 'continental day' is something of a misnomer. There is not a uniform way of organizing the school day in Europe. Most countries in the EEC actually have morning and afternoon sessions (e.g. Holland, Belgium and Spain), and some have a mix of days, with mornings only on some days and morning and afternoon sessions on others. School days also vary between regions within countries, and according to the age of children. Perhaps the country with a system closest to the popular view of the 'continental day' is West Germany. School starts at 8.00 am. and generally ends at 12.00 or 13.00 (information from Moss, 1988).

A system organized along West German lines could work well in this country. But it is important to note that much of its success would depend on the quantity and quality of care provided after the morning session was finished. Not only would the comments that have been made in Chapter 4 about lunchtime supervision still apply, but there would also have to be investment in the afternoon supervision. In Sweden, for example, this is provided by trained staff in separate, well-resourced centres.

But the main worry, of course, about the continental day – or indeed, as mentioned above, any shortening of the school day – is the problems it poses for working parents, who will have to face, and perhaps finance, childcare arrangements for the afternoon. Strong opposition from parents was one main reason why Avon

LEA shelved its plans to introduce the continental day into schools. Single parents in particular might have to give up work, and this could adversely affect their lives, as well as put extra burdens on social security. An earlier start to the school day in the morning might also cause problems; for example, children would need to, but might not, get to bed an hour earlier in order to get adequate sleep, and this might aggravate the already recognized problem of tiredness affecting children's work at school. Parents might also face a more difficult job in getting children to school in the morning, and, fathers in particular, may not get to see so much of them.

It is also worth pointing out the basic fact that if children stay on much beyond mid-day at school they are going to have to have a lunch – it cannot simply be ignored, or the responsibility for providing for it left to chance. There is already concern about the diet of many children in the country, partly brought about by the government's relinquishing of nutritional standards at the time of encouraging authorities to put out school meals services to private tender. There must be concern for children's health if opportunities for a meal at lunchtime become even more difficult. It is ironic that at a time in Britain when the traditional school dinner is less and less secure, and requirements about nutritional standards have been scrapped, other countries in Europe (e.g. Luxembourg and Spain) are moving toward the provision of meals and supervision at lunchtime.

There could be another problem if the school day simply ended much earlier than at present. Though one way of avoiding behaviour problems at playtime might be to shorten or do without, if this means children are leaving school much earlier, without adequate supervision, it will simply be transferring behaviour problems from the school premises to potentially more menacing ones in the street or the home. It may ease strains within schools but it may be creating them elsewhere. We come back to a main point: simply cutting down playtime is not adequate, unless there is a good deal of attention paid, and resources made available for, care after school.

There is another point as well. Although staff are often hard pressed to defend lunchtime in schools, it is a central fixture in the school day, and most have grown used to it. I suspect many would be uncomfortable about not having a lunchbreak with the children in the school, and not having an afternoon session. It would undoubtedly change the character of school life. Given that changes to the school day may be under increasing scrutiny in the future, it is worth quoting the cautionary words of a head who, after thought, defended the traditional school day. He probably speaks for many.

> When all is said and done I like having them around in the middle of the day. Dinner time is one opportunity for the total education of children – where we can teach social graces. We can help children who need to know that they can't shout and grab. It has the potential for a nice part of the school day. I'd like to see *more* of a family atmosphere. It gives us a chance to see children play and gives them a chance to see us (out of the classroom). There's also the possibility of extra curricular activities. I like the school day as it is. I like the afternoon period. It is valuable to see it as a full day at school – an important part of their lives. With the continental day there's likely to be less feeling for the school, and by the school – less of a unit, less of a family . . . if we didn't have a major break together. I recognize problems of lunchtime but we need to deal with the problems – as part of social care.

Again there are unlikely to be general solutions. Much resistance to change in the school day is no doubt attributable to tradition, and the inertia that can cause. But, as we have seen, there are some very real practical problems. And, as was evident in the words of the head just quoted, there are worries that the social and caring role of school would be affected. That such worries are not easily articulated or quantified, should not detract from their validity. What seems clear is that changes to the school day will have to be accompanied by attention to problems that might come about as a result, for example, the care of children when the school day finishes much earlier than at present. As more schools adopt changes to the school day, more information will be available upon which to make firmer judgements. It will take some time, though, to disentangle effects of changes to the school day on family life and children's education.

7
Conclusions

In this book some serious problems with playtime have been identified. We saw in Chapter 2 that there is a widespread view among teaching staff that children's behaviour in the playground is not as good as it might be. It can be desultory and gratuitously aggressive. The quality of play is not high and traditional games and rhymes are seen to be in decline. There can be particular problems for girls and the youngest children in school. Aggressive behaviour and name-calling, associated with children's ethnic group, can occur.

We saw in Chapter 4 that there are particular problems at lunchtime. It is the longest break and yet supervision is now in the hands of mostly untrained and poorly paid supervisors. There is increasing strain on heads.

And we saw in Chapter 5 that there are serious misgivings about the playground environment itself, and fears that its visual drabness and lack of interest for children might itself be a main cause of bad behaviour.

It was said in Chapter 1 that this book has been written in the context of a growing recognition that serious thought must be given to the institution of playtime. A main conclusion is that this is unlikely to be fruitful if undertaken on a piecemeal basis. The 'success' of playtime is affected by many factors, some of which have been identified in this book. Any review of playtime in schools will have to take these on board. Over the past year or so I have received letters from heads, teachers and advisers, expressing concern about behaviour in their school playgrounds, and asking for information on how it can be improved. While one of course sympathizes with the concern, and with the desire to improve matters, it is hoped that this book has been able to show that there are unlikely to be simple 'off-the-shelf' solutions. The answer is unlikely to be found, as I suspect some would hope, in a handout to be circulated at an INSET meeting.

In this book some possible improvements have been identified. There is a role for all concerned with playtime in schools. There is a contribution to be made by staff within schools – heads, teachers and dinner supervisors, as well as parents and governors – and also those outside – LEA administrators and advisers and Government officials. By way of summarizing suggested improvements to playtime, I look first at what can be done within schools. This is of particular relevance to heads, both because of their leadership role in their schools and also because much of the information I base these recommendations on came from discussions with them.

Initiatives within schools

Misbehaviour in the playground

1 A basic feature of an effective approach towards playground behaviour is a clearly articulated set of rules and sanctions (p.32). The aim should be to provide a framework within which children, teachers and supervisors are clear about what is unacceptable. A clearly defined hierarchy of sanctions seems to develop a sense of the severity of wrong doing.
2 Persistently bad behaviour and bullying need to be dealt with. Careful monitoring of day-to-day behaviour, with feedback to parents, should help. Some imaginative schemes were examined in Chapter 3. These could involve giving aggressors responsibilities for the smooth running of playtime, for example, appointing them as playground monitors or giving them responsibility for the well-being during playtime of their erstwhile victims.
3 A concern with unacceptable behaviour needs to be supplemented by a stress on encouraging positive behaviour in the playground (p.34). Persistent wrong-doers can be helped by a

careful programme of monitoring, praise and feedback.

4 Most effective will be a 'whole school' approach (see Chapter 3): 'whole school' also in the sense of involving all in school – head, teachers, supervisors, and if possible parents – in the creation and implementation of rules in the playground;
'whole school' also in the sense of not isolating the playground but working towards a policy on behaviour over the whole school day within which playtime is one part.

5 It is very important to look at, and act on, forms of inequality and abuse in the playground. As shown in Chapter 3 (p.40 to p.42) it is very difficult to affect gender-related behaviour. Understanding girls' and boys' viewpoints on contentious activities like football is a necessary starting point.

6 Racism in the playground will not go away in the absence of policies to combat it. I believe that racism and sexism, like other forms of abuse, can best be approached by a whole school policy (as defined above) based on an alternative moral position that offers non-retaliatory solutions to problems (see p.43)

Improving arrangements for playtime

Effective changes in playground behaviour can be brought about by altering arrangements for playtime. These could include:

1 Splitting and staggering playtimes (p.44).
2 Making separate arrangements for the youngest children in school (particularly newcomers to infant and first schools – see p.45).
3 Attending to the mix of year groups in the playground at the same time (p.46)
4 Considering entry into school from the playground at the beginning of the day (p.48).
5 Looking at entry into school from the playground (particularly lining up and queuing – see p.49).

Improving the quality of play

1 We also need to consider *what* activities children can do in the playground. Provision could be made to take out games equipment into the playground, perhaps on a loan and return basis (see p.51).

2 Staff could work with children to encourage cooperative games in the playground. This could be introduced during assembly, by classroom projects on playground games, and by encouraging children to show each other, and pass on, playground games (see p.52). A balance has to be struck between adult domination and neglect of play. Adults could work towards a 'catalyst' role in children's play. The bottom line is to take an *interest* in children's playground activities (see p.52 to 54).

Involving children in decisions about the playground

At the end of Chapter 3 I described two schemes to illustrate what could be done to improve playtime. The first was a cross-curricular project on playtime that helped get children and staff thinking in fundamental and imaginative ways about the use that could be made of the playground (p.56). The second was a children's council – an embryonic form of democratic working that offered one practical way of giving children a real voice in decisions about the school and playground life.

Both schemes had as a main ingredient what seems to be just about the most important step in improving playground behaviour; that is, they create conditions through which children's feelings about the playground can find expression, and can influence in real ways decisions about the playground. There are implications here that extend beyond the playground. Because of children's inside knowledge about playtime, it is a good subject through which to begin to involve them in meaningful participation in the community.

Improving supervision at lunchtime

1 Teaching staff should acquaint lunchtime supervisors with school policies on behaviour. Better still, supervisors should be involved in the creation of school policy, and be seen to have responsibility for carrying it out (see p.73 to 74).
2 Efforts should be made to increase liaison between teaching staff and lunchtime supervisors. This could be done by setting up, and giving direction to, meetings, but also altering arrangements

within school, for example, providing time after the dinner break when teaching and supervisory staff can both be in the classroom to discuss regularly children's behaviour and progress (see p.74).

3 Efforts should be made to train supervisors. While resources outside school could help (see below) there is much that could be done within schools. In Chapter 4, I identified four main areas that could be covered by training – child development, strategies for the management of children, knowledge of LEA and school policies, and health and safety. An important contribution could be made by senior teaching staff working directly with supervisors on the job, as it were (p.75).

Much 'training' would involve making explicit to supervisors what teachers often hold implicitly, for example about the value of play, cooperative learning and techniques of control.

Improving the playground environment

Aggressive and desultory behaviour in the playground may be symptoms of an uninteresting and barren environment. In Chapter 5 I reviewed some ways the playground could be improved.

1 Playground game markings are often predictable and unused. There could be periodic discussions with children about their use. Better still, children could be involved in their design and implementation (p.81 to 84).
2 One way of catering for different and often competing activities in the playground is to divide it up into separate areas. Examination of a drawing to scale should help to clarify the best use of space (see 84 to 85).
3 Playgrounds are often drab and sight lines severe. The contrast with primary school classrooms – which are often colourful and stimulating, is marked. Efforts should be made to make the playground more attractive, for example, by working on murals, putting out plants, creating attractive areas for waiting parents, and installing litter bins.
4 Perhaps the most obvious improvement to the playground is to install interesting permanent play equipment. Cost and safety are major obstacles. Careful thought needs to be given to what effects equipment will have on children's play. Single, large and expensive items may not necessarily improve play (see pp.89 to 98).

5 The playground is usually seen as a setting for a short recreational break. An alternative view is to consider ways it could be a learning environment that could extend and complement classroom experiences. This could involve the creation of conservation and wildlife areas. The exciting work in one infant school was described in Chapter 5 as a model of what could be achieved when the playground is considered as an educational resource, examined with the same care as that given to the classroom.

A policy on playtime

Taking all these possible improvements together therefore shows that there are many aspects to improving playtime, and that asking partial questions about anti-social behaviour is likely to receive partial answers. Such answers might help in the short term, but they are unlikely to improve playtime in a fundamental way. What is required is a fundamental rethink about playtime in the context of the way children's time is spent at school. An important conclusion I would draw is that for every school there needs to be a policy on playtime, in the same way that there are policies for reading, maths, science and so on. This does not mean that every school would end up with the same policy. Indeed it is likely that each would need to be different. Every one has to work out for themselves what best suits their playground, their educational policies, and their children and staff. But it must be thought out.

It must be recognized that this is not a choice between doing nothing or having a policy on playtime. Doing nothing is a policy, by default as it were, because children will interact in, and adapt to, whatever playground environment they find themselves in. The task is therefore to clarify and make explicit one's attitude to playtime and the playground.

Consideration of the points listed above should provide the basis for a policy on playtime. There are also several general considerations that might guide such an initiative. A central question to ask is what playtime is for, and one needs to evaluate what playtime provides for children. If it is thought that children and staff benefit from playtime – for example that children need to let off steam, and get value out of play, by learning rhymes and meeting friends from other classes – that is of course a legitimate view. But one needs to check to see that these objectives are being met. How many can truthfully say they have looked closely at what happens in the playground? We need to take more interest in what happens there. The process in schools of highlighting playtime as a subject for serious attention may itself help clarify strategies, for example, to such problems as anti-social behaviour in the playground. It should help decide on priorities amongst various paths towards improvement – some of which have been reviewed above. For example, it might be felt that anti-social behaviour is a function of design features in the playground and best dealt with by alterations to the environment. It might also be decided that supervision at break times is not satisfactory, and ways of improving the quality of care need to be sought.

Play itself should be taken seriously. It would probably be true to say that staff in most schools send children out to the playground without giving much thought to what happens there. The contrast with the amount of preparation and thought given to classroom activities is marked. But it is not just a distinction between work and play. The contrast is also marked between play in the playground, on the one hand, and the amount of attention that has been paid to the role of play in children's early learning experiences, and how children's play can be enhanced on the other hand. Much has now been written on play, especially with regard to children of pre-school age. It is a central part of the nursery curriculum, and nursery staff have much expertise in the way play can, for example, enhance linguistic and conceptual development, and how it can be integrated with more formal activities. And yet here are children, some of whom were in the nursery a month or so ago, being sent out to survive in the playground without thought or resources given to what they might do there! It is the one part of the school day when we seem to fail in our responsibilities as educators.

It is helpful to consider the playground in the context of the different areas of the school curriculum. We saw in Chapter 5 some ways in which the playground could be used as an educational resource, to extend work in the classroom. This has involved initiatives like a nature garden or pond. Valuable though these can be, one could go further, in order to look for other ways the playground can extend educational experiences. One direction would be for work on children's oral and written language development to take on board the kinds of language used in the playground.

Sitton and Jeter (1980) have argued that there is much of educational value in integrating children's 'folklore' into formal classroom settings; for example, children's play forms can open doors to the enjoyment of literature and to self-confidence in the use of language, and also to cross cultural sharing and appreciation. The authors describe how teachers can become collectors of children's folklore – perhaps producing a tape of collected songs and rhymes – and how this can be used in the classroom, for example to encourage children to collect and 'publish' their own material. They call their work the 'Pass it On' project.

It is important to stress again the key role of involving pupils in improvements to playtime. This applies to the different types of improvement described in this book, for example, to the quality of their play behaviour, to the playground environment, including game markings, and to rules of conduct in the playground. Policies on playtime will be successful to the extent that pupils' behaviour is affected, and this is likely to be most fundamentally achieved if staff and pupils work cooperatively toward solutions. Pupils are the exclusive consumers, as it were, of the playground, and policies are unlikely to work well, or last long, if pupils do not have a commitment to them.

How might improvements to playtime be started? The first and most important step is to look at what happens at the moment in the playground. In general, adults seem very uninformed. One starting point for any initiative, therefore, could be observation conducted in a systematic fashion by someone in the playground, in order to see what is really happening and to try to identify problem areas. It might involve the use of time sampling and other techniques (see Croll, 1986). Use might also be made of rating scales in order to evaluate in a detailed way what the playground has to offer. (An example of such a scale can be found in Lovell and Harms (1985).) GRIST funds might be used to help with this kind of work in the playground.

Again, pupils might be involved, at the beginning of an initiative on playtime. A teacher in Cardiff has described how she got her class to look in detail at the playground (M. Evans, 1986). She first of all asked the children to remember what they could about the place they used every day. She found that they remembered very little. And so they went to the playground to look, and then on their return to the classroom they talked about, and drew, the playground. Other work followed, for example measuring of the playground, and recording of colours, sounds and insect life. On the last day of the summer term the children presented their findings to the rest of the school and showed pictures of the games they played. It is easy to see how useful this kind of exploratory work could be in attempts to improve the playground. The initial work, done by the children, can both inform and extend their class work, and also create an informed basis for, and commitment to, efforts to improve the playground.

Support from outside schools

A lot can therefore be done to improve schools through initiatives within schools. If the changes recommended above were applied in a methodical fashion then improvements in playground behaviour should take place. But we have also seen that much could be done to support those in schools.

There is much more that could be done at the LEA level.

1 Perhaps the most important contribution is to offer school staff support in the carrying out of initiatives to improve and rethink playtime, along the lines suggested above.
2 School staff could be helped to work through improvements, perhaps inviting speakers with experience of playground improvements to visit schools and discuss what could be done.
3 LEA staff could set up projects to involve children and staff in the design and laying down of playground markings.
4 They could set up and monitor training packages for lunchtime supervisors. This is done in some LEAs but much more could be done. One suggestion is to provide videos of playground incidents for discussion, or even whole training packages on video (see p.78).

Work can be done within individual schools but, as suggested in Chapter 3, it is likely to be most effective if it is part of a wider LEA initiative, for example on behaviour in school and playground.

There is a clear need for more advice to staff about improvements that can be made. There are advisory bodies and voluntary organizations who can help with specific aspects of the playground, usually with improvements to the physical environment. Some of these are described in Chapter 5. In particular, the Learning Through Landscapes Project should help provide valuable guidance to schools. But, in line with a main argument of this chapter, school staff are likely to require a general strategy for improving playtime, that takes in the environment, but also includes ways of dealing with misbehaviour, ways of enhancing the creative aspects of play, and strategies for lunchtime and wet play. Improvements to playtime require long-term strategic planning that cuts across a range of initiatives, and many staff at present are unclear where they can go for help. Such advice does not seem to fit easily into the existing LEA advisory service. It seems clear that someone within the education service needs to be given direct responsibility for improvements to playtime and playgrounds. Improvements should not be left entirely to individual schools. Advisory services outside LEAs that provided integrated, overall advice on playtime would also have many customers!

Extra resources

Much could be achieved in schools and LEAs within existing budgets. But, as I showed in Chapter 5, there are worries about playtime that involve solutions that require extra resources. For example, providing adequately for safety in playgrounds after the installation of equipment requires resources beyond that which many individual schools can raise.

Another important concern, as we saw in Chapter 4, is that of supervision at lunchtime. It is difficult to see how improvements can occur without extra resources. This could take at least two directions. First, more resources would allow improvements in the pay and prestige of supervisors. This would help make the job more attractive, would attract better candidates, and help improve the quality of supervisors. We saw that problems of behaviour could be caused by pupils and parents not having respect for supervisors. As was said in Chapter 4, it is an important post and provisions for it must be taken more seriously. At the moment we are expecting quality supervision on the cheap.

Extra resources could also be used to increase the numbers of supervisors at lunchtime. We saw that heads sometimes felt, with the numbers of supervisors allowed them, that the main priority was simply to survive until the afternoon period began. At very least there should be enough supervisors to allow one for every class in the school. We saw that this could help improve relationships with teachers and children, and make 'wet' playtimes safer and easier to supervise.

Secondly, more resources are required for the training of supervisors. Some main features of such training were described in Chapter 4. This is an essential part of the necessary upgrading of the supervisors' job. Much can be done within schools, as we have seen, but it is difficult to see great progress being made if there is not a wider commitment to training, and this will required resources to back it up.

There is currently concern in schools that the money earmarked for lunchtime supervisors, rather than being increased, might in fact be cut. At the time of writing (late 1988) it seems that the Education Secretary, Kenneth Baker, has scrapped plans to reduce the level of grant for mid-day supervision next year, and instead plans to get rid of it altogether, maintaining that mid-day supervision is sufficiently well-established for it to be supported through mainstream funding to local authorities. This seems optimistic, at a time when LEAs are very hard pressed to meet existing commitments, let alone the funds that will be required to meet Mr Baker's own initiatives in the Education Reform Act. In the light of all that has been said in this book about the need to increase resources at lunchtime, this is a regrettable step, and it is clear that the message from schools about lunchtime supervision has not got through. Once again, it appears as if playtime is being conveniently overlooked. It is surely wrong for lunchtime to depend on the exploitation of head's goodwill, and the use of cheap labour. It is also short-sighted because, as we have seen again and again in this book, playtime experiences affect the quality of education overall. There are also opportunities to enhance the quality of the whole school experience.

Another development with implications for playtime is the government's plans for Local Financial Management in Schools, contained in the Education Reform Act of 1988. Whatever the overall merit or not of school staff having responsibility for their own budget, there is cause for concern if it results in less resources for supervision at lunchtime. Headteachers and governors will be faced with difficult decisions about priorities, at present faced by LEAs. If heads do not see supervision as a priority they may try to maintain it at present, or even reduced, levels. This would be regrettable. It may also result in wide differences between schools in resources allocated to ancillary staff. On the other hand, headteachers, as we saw in Chapter 4, are often also keenly aware of the importance of playtime.

In future it may be that we need to look carefully and fundamentally at alternatives to existing arrangements for employment of supervisors at lunchtime. We have seen that the supervisor's post has low prestige, low pay, and inconvenient hours. An adequate supply depends on the presence of women in the margins of the labour market. It seems likely that more and more women will seek full-time, or better part-time, jobs, as in other countries in Europe, and so the numbers of women willing to take on lunchtime supervision may well shrink. In this context, one needs to review the whole structure of the employment of workers in schools. One alternative model would be to consider linking the roles of after-school and mid-day supervision. This might help to concentrate resources, and build up expertise in the non-teaching care of children, as well as provide more attractive supervisory posts. At present, for example in Haringey LEA, after-school care is provided by a separate department to education. It might make sense to consider ways in which after school and lunchtime care could be combined.

Alternatives to playtime

But if there are problems with fixed period playtime, and these seem after careful thought to be insurmountable, then we should not be shy about considering possible alternatives. This consideration is likely to happen more and more, for reasons explained in Chapter 6, but there is a danger it too will be done in a piecemeal fashion, and not in the context of a wider debate on the advantages of different schemes. The central point of such a debate must be the effect on children's education. The experience of staff at a South London school (see Chapter 6) suggests that a school day without any fixed period playtime can work well, to the advantage of children's school experience, but that it depends intimately on a clear and agreed view among school staff about how children learn. Changes in arrangements that are not accompanied by such a clarity of purpose are likely to be just disruptive, and may well be short-lived.

It is also probable that the 'continental day' will come more into deliberations. As discussed in Chapter 6, this arrangement could work, but it requires adequate resourcing of after-school care for children. A school day that extended from 8 to 1, followed by lunch on site, and then other activities in the afternoon, might look like a good arrangement, but present arrangements for lunchtime show that it could be disastrous for children if it is attempted on the cheap, without a fundamental look at the quality of after-school supervision. Much of the impetus for the 'continental day' has come from the supposed advantages of arrangements in other countries in Europe. But it should be recognized that the training and funding of non-teaching staff in schools is often taken more seriously there.

Where to now?

There are, therefore, messages in this book about playtime for staff within schools, LEAs and government. There are also messages for future research. In my view there are three areas which need to be developed.

The first is the need, as shown in Chapter 2, for detailed study of playground behaviour, that would pay particular attention to aggressive and anti-social behaviour – its origins and consequence in the playground – and to the different use of the playground by boys and girls. As we saw in Chapter 2, strong views are held about playground behaviour, but these are far in advance of any good data about just what is going on. Such a study should aim to provide results that would inform efforts to improve playtime for children.

A second direction would be to evaluate and compare different arrangements for playtime. We have looked in this book at initiatives that sound interesting and challenging, but there is very little objective evidence by which others might assess their effect iveness, and what implications there might be for steps that could be taken. For example, little is known in Britain about the effect on children's behaviour of changes to the physical environment of the playground. Is it the case that 'contemporary' playgrounds, with colourful and flexible equipment, and a well-stocked nature garden, have a noticeable effect on the quality of children's play? What effect does the implementation of a whole school policy on a code of conduct have on behaviour in the playground? Are there positive effects on relationships within school? What long-term effects are found on the quality of play after a concerted effort to get children involved in their playground activities? What are the long-term effects of an initiative on the use of playground game markings? The scrapping of all fixed period playtime is a bold move, that some have no doubt contemplated, but further evidence is required on how it affects children's behaviour, and how it is viewed by staff and children.

And, finally, a third direction is to look at playtime from an international perspective. There is much to be learnt from other countries about how they arrange for supervision of playtime and after school activities, as well as alternatives to the way the school day is organized. There are likely to be lessons there for Britain.

A final word

My main objective in writing this book has been to show that a concern with playtime is overdue and necessary. I have tried to promote playtime and the use of playgrounds as topic for serious debate. I hope enough has been said to justify this aim and offer some guidelines for the debate. Throughout I have tried to identify problems and look for improvements. Paradoxically, the current turmoil in education may serve to bring into focus previously neglected parts of the school day, including playtime. But whatever the effect of wider debates in education, I feel confident that the concern with playtime will grow and develop. The response to my work, and other work on playtime, by teachers, administrators, the media and parents convinces me we are on to an important topic. In this area at least I feel hopeful. I see this book as a start, and there is much to be done. I am sure it will be possible to write a very different one ten years hence.

References

ALLAN, P. (1986). 'Islington schools environment project', *School and Community*, 46, Autumn.

AUSTIN, R. (1986). 'The dividing line', *Junior Education*, 10, 11, November.

BAKER, D. (1977). 'Worlds of play', *Childhood Education*, March, 245–249.

BAKER, N. (1987). 'Labour of love', *Times Educational Supplement*, 6 March.

BEAUMANOR RESEARCH GROUP (1985) Survey into playtimes and playgrounds. Unpublished report.

BETH-HALAACHMY, S. (1980). 'Elementary schoolchildren's behaviour during school recess period' In: WILKINSON, P. (Ed.) *In Celebration of Play*. London: Croom Helm.

BHATIA, S. (1987). 'Up the wall', *Child Education*, May, p.23.

BLATCHFORD, P., BATTLE, S. and MAYS J. (1982). *The First Transition: Home to Preschool*. Windsor: NFER-NELSON.

BLATCHFORD, P., BURKE, J., FARQUHAR, C., PLEWIS, P. and TIZARD, B. (1987). 'A systematic observation study of children's behaviour at infant school', *Research Papers in Education*, 2, 1, 47–62.

BLATCHFORD, P. (1988). 'Girls and girls come out to play?' *AMMA Report*, 10, 8, 2–3.

BOWERS, L. (1979). 'Toward a science of playground design: principles of design for play centers for all children', *Journal of Physical Education and Recreation*, 50, 8, 51–54.

BROWN, J. G. and BURGER, C. (1984). 'Playground designs and preschool children's behaviour', *Environment and Behaviour*, 16, 5, 599-626.

BRUNER, J. S., JOLLY, A. and SILVA, K. (Eds) (1976). *Play – Its Role in Development and Evolution*. Harmondsworth: Penguin Education.

CHAPPELL, H. (1986). 'The concrete jungle', *New Society*, 19 September.

CHILD EDUCATION (1987). 'A World of Games', May 1987.

CLEAVE, S., JOWETT, S. and BATE, M. (1982), . . . *And So To School: A Study of Continuity from Pre-School to Infant School*. Windsor: NFER-NELSON.

COMMUNITY SERVICE VOLUNTEERS (1980). *Making Playgrounds*. 237 Pentonville Road, London N1 9NJ.

COTLER, H. (1980). 'It's pouring . . . but not necessarily boring', *Instructor*, April, 56–60.

CROLL, P. (1986), *Systematic Classroom Observation*. Lewes: Falmer.

DOROJAIYE, S. M. (1977). 'Children's traditional games and rhymes in three cultures', *Educational Research*, 19, 3, 223–226.

DUNN, S. and MORGAN, V. (1987). 'Nursery and infant school play patterns; some related differences', *British Educational Research Journal*, 13, 3, 271–282.

EVANS, M. (1986). 'Language development and the playground', *School and Community*, 46, Autumn.

FOWLER, S. A., DOUGHERTY, K. C., KIRBY, K. C. and KOHLER, F. W. (1986). 'Role reversals: an analysis of therapeutic effects achieved with disruptive boys during their appointments as peer monitors', *Journal of Behaviour Analysis*, 19, 4, 437–444.

GALTON, M., SIMON, B. and CROLL, P. (1980). *Inside the Primary Classroom*. London: Routledge and Kegan Paul.

GREAT BRITAIN. DEPARTMENT OF EDUCATION AND SCIENCE (1987). *School Teachers' Pay and Conditions Document*. London: HMSO.

HART, C. H. and SHEENAN, R. (1986). 'Preschoolers' play behaviour in outdoor environments: effects of traditional and contemporary playgrounds', *American Education Research Journal*, 23, 4, 668–678.

HESELTINE, P. and HOLBORN, J. (1988). *Playgrounds: Planning design and Construction of Play Environment*. London: Mitchell.

INDEPENDENT, THE, 9 June 1988 (news item).
ILEA (INNER LONDON EDUCATION AUTHORITY) (1986). *Primary Matters: Some Approaches to Equal Opportunities in Primary Schools*. London: ILEA.
ILEA (INNER LONDON EDUCATION AUTHORITY). 'Playtime Project', ILEA NEWS, 3 March 1987.
KELLY, E. (1988). 'Pupils, racial groups and behaviour in schools'. In: KELLY, E. and COHEN, T. (Eds) *Racism in Schools – New Research Evidence*. Stoke-on-Trent: Trentham.
KELLY, J. (in press). Modifying children's individual and group behaviour at breaktimes: two case studies.
LOVELL, P. and HARMS, T. (1985). 'How can playgrounds be improved?: a rating scale', *Young Children*, March.
MARES, C. and STEPHENSON, R. (1987). *Inside Outside: an Action Plan for Improving the Primary School Environment.* Keep Britain Tidy Group Schools Research Project, Brighton Polytechnic.
MOSS, P. (1988). *Child Care and Equality of Opportunity: Consolidated Report to the European Commission.* London Commission of the European Commodities.
MURPHY, H. A., HUTCHINSON, J. M. and BAILEY, J. S. (1983). 'Behavioural school psychology goes outdoors: the effect of organised games on playground aggression', *Journal of Applied Behaviour Analysis*, 16, 29–35.
NATIONAL PLAYING FIELDS ASSOCIATION (1983). The Great Play Time Games Kit, 25 Ovington Square, London SW3 PLJ.
NICKELL, P. and KENNEDY, M. (1987). 'Global perspectives through children's games. How to do it', *Social Education*, 51, 3, 1–8 March.
OLWEUS, D. (1984) 'Aggressors and their victims: bullying at school'. In: FRUDE, N. and GAULT, H. (Eds) *Disruptive Behaviour in Schools.* Chichester: Wiley.
OPIE, I. and OPIE, P. (1969). *Children's Games in Street and Playground.* London: Oxford University Press.
ORLICK, T. (1979). *Cooperative Sports and Games Books: Challenge Without Competition.*
PALMER, P. (1975). 'Rhyme, rhythm and song', *Times Educational Supplement*, 30 October.
PARNELL, K. and KETTERSON, P. (1980). 'What should a playground offer?', *The Elementary School Journal*, 80, 5, 233–238

PHELPS, P. (1984). 'Creative playgrounds for the pre-school children', *Early Child Development and Care*, 17, 23–36.

POOLE, G. S. and POOLE, B. L. (1982). 'Parks and playgrounds as adjunct classrooms', *Parks and Recreation*, 17, 9, 63–66.

ROBERTS, A. (1979). 'The games French children play', *New Society*, 2 August.

SCHOOL CURRICULUM DEVELOPMENT COMMITTEE: EQUAL OPPORTUNITIES COMMISSION (SCOC) (1987). *'Genderwatch!'*

SHARP, C. (1988). 'Starting school at four', *Research Papers in Education*, 3, 1, 64–90.

SITTON, T. and JETER, J. (1980). 'Discovering children's folklore', *Teacher*, March, 58–61.

SLUCKIN, A. (1981). *Growing Up in the Playground*. London: Routledge and Kegan Paul.

STADLEN, F. (1974). 'Mudpies or grand design: it's imagination that counts', *Times Educational Supplement*, 3 March.

STEPHENSON, P. and SMITH, D. (1989). 'Bullying in the junior school'. In: TATTUM, D. P. and LANE, O. A. (Eds) *Bullying in Schools*. Stoke-on-Trent: Trentham.

TATTUM, D. P. and LANE, O. A. (Eds) 1989.*Bullying in Schools*. Stoke-on-Trent: Trentham.

THE LEISURE MANAGER (1986). 'Safety in playgrounds', 4, 2 February.

TIMES EDUCATIONAL SUPPLEMENT (TES), 30 November 1984. 'Boredom, bruises and brrr . . . that's break.'

TIMES EDUCATIONAL SUPPLEMENT (TES), 6 November 1987. 'Showing the yellow card.'

TIMES EDUCATIONAL SUPPLEMENT (TES), 8 January 1988. 'Play Safe.'

TIZARD, B., BLATCHFORD, P., BURKE, J., FARQUHAR, C. and PLEWIS, I. (1988). *Young Children At School in the Inner City*. Hove: Lawrence Erlbaum Associates.

WALDEN, R. and WALKERDINE, V. (1985). *Girls and Mathematics: From Primary to Secondary Schooling*. Bedford Way Papers, Institute of Education, University of London, No. 24.

WATSON, V. and TIPP, G. (1983). *Impact Absorbing Surfaces for Children's Playgrounds*. London: National Playing Fields Association.

WHICH? (1988). 'Safety in playgrounds'. April, 1988.

WHITE, P. (1988). 'The Playground project: a democratic learning experience'. In: LAUDER, H. and BROWN, P. (Eds) *Education in Search of A Future*. London: Falmer.

WHOLF, F. (1984). 'Playground PALs', *Instructor*, May, 46–48.

Index